THE ELIZABETHAN MISCELLANIES

THE ELIZABETHAN
MISCELLANIES

Their Development and Conventions

By Elizabeth W. Pomeroy

UNIVERSITY OF CALIFORNIA PRESS

BERKELEY · LOS ANGELES · LONDON

1973

University of California Publications
English Studies: 36

Approved for publication October 29, 1971
Issued February 14, 1973

University of California Press
Berkeley and Los Angeles
California

◇

University of California Press, Ltd.
London, England

ISBN: 0-520-09438-7

Library of Congress Catalog Card No.: 76-185978

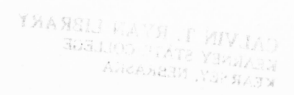

FOR CHARLES

PREFACE

IN THEIR OWN TIME, the Elizabethan miscellanies were popular, abundant, and often influential on one another and on wider poetic practice. They were widely read, often reprinted, and sometimes denounced; but interest in them never flagged. From *Tottel's Miscellany* in 1557 (preceded by the now fragmentary *Court of Venus* from perhaps the 1530s) to *A Poetical Rhapsody* in 1602, they were a continuous presence.

Yet modern readers of the period are surprisingly unfamiliar with the miscellanies, and no bibliography has yet recorded their full number without omission or error. Their varied interests for present scholars remain largely unexplored. The collections shed light on the history of taste and on the directions of change in poetic theme and technique. Their story reveals the practices of a flourishing book trade and patterns of imitation and interaction between poets and poetic types. Literary conventions passed in and out of their development, shaping one volume or filling out substance in another. Yet of the many questions they raise, only one, perhaps the least fruitful, has been pursued at all: identification of the authors of the many anonymous poems. The miscellanies have not been assessed as a phenomenon or as a form; nor have their gatherings of poetry been studied in particular literary contexts.

For some years texts of the anthologies were imperfect and difficult to find, but in recent decades the most important of them have been meticulously edited by Hyder E. Rollins. With the textual work virtually completed, these are now ready for close critical attention.

As an introduction to the miscellanies, my study has two purposes: to show the development of the form throughout

Elizabeth's reign, the volumes all to some extent the progeny of *Tottel's Miscellany,* yet varying widely in content and purpose; and to suggest, through discussions of four individual collections, critical approaches to the miscellanies as poetic wholes. For the first time all the collections are described and placed in historical sequence, providing a complete perspective of the form.

I have been content with brief summaries of textual problems, identities and backgrounds of authors or editors, sources for particular poems and for some whole collections, and other peripheral subjects. My concern has been to reintroduce the miscellanies by showing their development and by critically examining four distinctive examples. New questions are posed here as others are answered, showing that the miscellanies have inviting possibilities for further study.

For criticism and counsel at many points, I am grateful to Richard Lanham and especially to Paul Jorgensen and Hugh G. Dick, whose recent death has closed his wise and patient work of teaching. He will be remembered. The staff of the Huntington Library was unfailing in help and goodwill. Margaret Graham provided vital ground support for me, and Grace H. Stimson has edited the manuscript with careful skill.

My husband Charles neither typed my drafts, compiled the index, nor read the proofs. Nevertheless, he has made the whole enterprise possible. My daughter Margaret renewed my *élan,* and my son John was present at the creation. I thank them all.

CONTENTS

CHAPTER I

THE DEVELOPMENT OF THE MISCELLANIES TO 1590

I N 1557, the year of incorporation of the Stationers' Company and one year before Elizabeth's accession, Richard Tottel published *Songes and Sonnettes, written by the ryght honorable Lorde Henry Haward late Earle of Surrey, and other*. By 1587 this volume, known since the 1870 Arber reprint as *Tottel's Miscellany,* had gone through nine editions. It has long been accepted as a wellspring for the poetry that followed; according to Hyder E. Rollins, its modern editor, "adequately to discuss its influence would be almost to write a history of the first three decades of Elizabethan poetry."[1]

Less frequently noticed, however, have been the progeny of the miscellany itself, collections published throughout Elizabeth's reign which hoped to attract the interest awakened by *Songes and Sonnettes*. Some twenty volumes fall into this category, and several others are closely related. The term "miscellany," unknown in the sixteenth century, has always been used very loosely. In this study, following modern usage, it designates any printed volume of poetry having three or more authors, even collections ascribed to a single author but now suspected or known to be by several. Excluded are volumes not entirely in English, songbooks containing music, and collected works of a writer prefaced by commendatory poems. Some miscellanies here considered contain some prose, but all are predominantly poetry. The survey ends with the death of Elizabeth in 1603.[2]

The anthologies were so popular that one was being printed or reprinted in almost every year of the reign, and evidence suggests that even more editions have been lost. They reveal much about the period: the shifting, and sometimes the stubbornness, of public taste; the closeness of courtly and popular forms; the vitalizing influence of music; the sobering element of moral concern; the vigor of meters emerging from fifteenth-century uncertainty. Once *Tottel's Miscellany* was established as a model, other literary forms of the day cast their influence here and there among the progeny. Broadside ballads, psalm translations, epigrams recovered from the classics, vestiges of medieval tragedy, current versions of allegory—all appear in the background of one or another miscellany.

The anthologies themselves arose from a combination of circumstances. Since most poets did not seek publication, lovers of poetry copied favorite verses from the manuscript pages that freely circulated. The many extant commonplace books establish the popularity of this fashion.[3] A collector with taste and a lively literary acquaintance could create a potentially successful miscellany by his own choices. In this way, undoubtedly, some volumes came wholly, or in large part, directly into a printer's hands. Sometimes an editor or a compiler consciously gathered poems to print, following the custom many were practicing as a fashionable habit. Since an author had no rights in a circulating manuscript, publishers could glean as they chose. They might decide to omit or alter a poem's ascription if it served their purposes; frequently the author's name had been left out in an earlier recopying and the publisher was ignorant of it anyway. A poet sometimes expressed outrage to find his verses printed at all, or to see his name attached to another man's work. He could only protest, hoping to have explanations and retractions printed at a later time.

Publishers resorted to other frauds to court popularity. Besides puffing a title page with a famous name, often of a poet who was only slightly connected with the volume, they might boast falsely of poems "never before imprinted" or try to pass off a later edition of a work as an entirely new one. Evidence of these practices will appear in the accounts that follow. Publishers were as shrewd in their tactics as the loose protective statutes for writers would then allow. In 1625 George Wither inveighed against the printer's ways:

He makes no scruple to put out the right Authors Name, & insert another in the second edition of a Booke; And when the impression of some pamphlet lyes upon his hands, to imprint new Titles for yt, (and so take mens moneyes twice or thrice, for the same matter under diverse names) is no iniury in his opinion. If he gett any written Coppy into his powre, likely to be vendible, whether the Author be willing or no, he will publish it; And it shall be contrived and named alsoe, according to his owne pleasure: which is the reason, so many good Bookes come forth imperfect, and with foolish titles.[4]

There were other sources for the poetry in the miscellanies. Novels, plays, broadsides, songbooks, or any printed work of the time could be raided as easily as manuscripts. And besides the commonplace books, *The Greek Anthology* provided a formal model for at least a few of the Elizabethan volumes. Meanwhile, poetical miscellanies had already appeared in Italy and may have been known to some collectors.[5]

The history of the Elizabethan miscellanies really begins before 1557. Some twenty years earlier, *The Court of Venus,* of which only three fragments now survive, appeared as the first lyric anthology of Tudor England. Despite its incompleteness the book raises historical and critical questions of interest to this study, and it was remembered throughout the century by imitators and critics. Russell Fraser, its modern editor, dates the fragments 1535–1539 (called Douce), 1547–1549 (Stark, which has the running title *A Boke of Balettes*) and 1561–1564 (Folger). An entry in the *Stationers' Register* for 1557 indicates another edition, now lost, and Fraser suggests evidence for yet another.[6] *The Court of Venus* contains a "Pilgrim's Tale" in extremely rough but vigorous couplets, a prologue, and fifteen amorous lyrics. All the poems are unsigned. The "Pilgrim's

Tale," ascribed in the sixteenth century to Chaucer, is earnest, anticlerical, and cryptic, with a puzzling use of political prophecy.[7] In the prologue, which has affinities with John Gower's *Confessio Amantis* (ca. 1390), a disconsolate lover is referred by Genius to Venus's court for redress. The lyrics are all in the manner of Wyatt, with his characteristic moments of detachment and ironic reflection. Five of the poems are surely his, three are probably his, and some or all of the other seven may be. Fraser in fact suggests that the entire section of short poems in the *Court* may have been devoted to Wyatt.[8]

Several points raised by *The Court of Venus* are especially interesting for the future history of the miscellanies. This collection, though retaining some old poetic fashions, also anticipates future developments. The "Pilgrim's Tale" imitates a Chaucerian tale, in cruder style; the prologue also has medieval roots, recalling the *Romance of the Rose* in its allegory and love heresy. The lyrics, whether Wyatt's or not, sound strikingly modern in contrast, as they do even when set against some Petrarchan laments written much later in the century. The lover of these poems defers to no metaphorical arbiter, but controls his experience largely by his own consciousness. Perhaps, as Miss Foxwell suggests, the prologue and Wyatt's songs were deliberately put together to show the old and new fashions in love poetry.[9] It is impossible to comment on the structure of this miscellany, since we have only parts and no knowledge of differences in the editions. But the mixture of styles must be noted. The same principle is used for diversity in *Brittons Bowre of Delights* (1591), *A Poetical Rhapsody* (1602), and others, and as a structural element in *The Phoenix Nest* (1593).

The combination of didactic and amorous verse in *The Court of Venus* also became a model. With few exceptions, later anthologies were miscellaneous in this respect as well as in authorship. Some clearly sought to gain a wider audience by presenting a variety of poems; others, like *The Paradise of Dainty Devices* (1576) and *England's Helicon* (1600), seem to have had narrower principles for selection. But the *Court,* at least as it is now known, contained predominantly love poetry, starting a dialectic of moral and amorous verse which continued through all the miscellanies. It was immediately and persistently attacked as ungodly and shameless, with its "songes of loue to the goddes of lechery."[10] A lost *Court of Venus Moralized* (1566–67), by Thomas Brice, took the most direct approach to neutralizing the evil (as, apparently, did his *Songes and Sonnettes,* 1567–68, also lost, an antidote to Tottel's collection). John Hall, pressed to further indignation by Tottel's volume of 1557, published in 1565 his *The Court of Virtue,* which does survive.[11] Although a single-author work, it has some notable similarities to the "profane," and genuine, miscellanies.

Hall's full title, *The Court of Virtue, Containing many holy or spiritual songs Sonnets psalms ballets short sentences as well of holy scriptures as others* &c, seems to allude to Tottel's miscellany, as well as the earlier *Court,* and it advertises diversity of kinds as the later collections frequently did. In recasting three poems by Wyatt, two of them from *The Court of Venus,* Hall turns the amorous lute to this sober use:

> My lute awake and prayse the lord,
> My heart and handes therto accord:
> Agreing as we haue begon,
> To syng out of gods holy word.
> And so procede tyll we haue done.

Like its counterpart, *The Court of Virtue* begins with a lengthy prologue, but here the poet meets the nine muses of Christian poetry in a dream vision and is bidden by lady Virtue to compile a book of holy songs. Since the element of music seemed to intensify the evil under attack, it may also recall men to a more godly mood:

> Suche as in carnall loue reioyce,
> Trim songes of loue they wyll compile,
> And synfully with tune and voyce
> They syng their songes in pleasant stile,
> To Venus that same strompet vyle....
>   A booke also of songes they haue,
> And Venus court they doe it name.
> No fylthy mynde a songe can craue,
> —But therein he may finde the same:
> And in suche songes is all their game.

Hall's dream urges him to compile

> Ryght sober songes godly and sadde,
> Compyled of gods holy lawes:
> of vertue and wyse olde sayd sawes....

His use of refrains and the frequent inclusion of short musical settings show the element of music operating for his own purposes.

The Court of Virtue consists of poems on Scripture, laments, and warnings. Its homiletic tone is directed toward a vast range of contemporary lore and life. The book was never reprinted, apparently; in contrast, *The Court of Venus* may have had as many as five editions. This disproportion, however, suggests little about the popularity of future volumes. Both didactic and amorous collections had strong public appeal and gained vigor from awareness of each other. A modern reader may wonder at the bitterness of the attacks on *The Court of Venus,* since its love poetry was hardly more scandalous than much that preceded it. Franklin Dickey suggests the novelty of print, and Lily Bess Campbell, the openness of the volume's title, as reasons for the sharp protests.[12] To the end of Elizabeth's reign it was the miscellany most often attacked by name. In any event, reaction is itself a stimulus, and later compilers apparently drew upon *The Court of Venus* both for allusions and for its established audience.[13] The popularity of *Tottel's Miscellany* was not without a foundation.

There was also an abundance of psalm translations in Tudor England, written partly to compete with the profane lyrics. A hundred and one editions of the Sternhold and Hopkins version of the Psalms were printed between 1549 and 1603. Clearly they were a familiar poetic presence. These metrical versions had several probable influences on later miscellany poetry: their moral gravity, their iambic meter, and the four-teeners so common in early Elizabethan verse. Wyatt, a courtly maker and also a translator of psalms, linked the two traditions at a time when both were achieving a wide public, but his love poetry in *Tottel's Miscellany* left an even more noted legacy than the Old Version Psalter.[14]

In 1577, the year that *Tottel's Miscellany* first appeared, its audience demanded two more printings, and there were six more by 1587.[15] The first seven were printed by Tottel, whose exact role as editor, and for which editions, is uncertain.[16] However, someone close to compiling the volume made the well-known emendations that presented Wyatt and Surrey in altered form to their contemporaries. The regularizing of Wyatt's meters and the fewer changes in Surrey's illustrate the freedom of publishers in printing manuscripts that came into their hands. The miscellany includes a total of 310 poems, in four sections devoted to Surrey, Wyatt, Grimald, and "un-certain authors." Among the latter can be identified Chaucer, Lord Vaux, John Heywood, Thomas Norton, Sir John Cheke, and others. Even John Hall, as irony would have it, found two of his poems here, taken from his *Proverbs of Salomon* (1550).[17]

The diversity of *Tottel's Miscellany* was a seedbed for miscel-lanies that followed. It includes sonnets, epigrams, epitaphs and elegies, satires, and pastoral and narrative poems. Courtly love has its expression, as do the admonitions of homiletic verse.

There are translations or imitations of the classics and translations of contemporary French and Italian originals. Like *The
Court of Venus,* Tottel's collection has both archaic and innovative elements, in meters, subjects, and poets. It also combines
amorous and didactic verse, with the proverbial commonplaces
and Petrarchan conceits that reappeared in many later volumes.
The closeness to music is here as well, with Wyatt's songs,
musical settings existing elsewhere for some of the poems, and
the publication of some as ballads. This variety proved to be a
treasury of merits freely drawn upon by the imitators who
followed.

Chronologically, the next work within the present definition
was the durable *Mirror for Magistrates,* first printed in 1559.[18]
It was, of course, not a lyric collection, and its complicated
career and growth have little bearing on the story of the genuine
miscellanies. Yet it does demonstrate the appeal of edifying
verse, cast in narrative form or sometimes in dramatic mono-
logue. This kind of extended didactic poetry, often with a
similar historical basis, recurred in later anthologies, providing
a formal contrast to the aphoristic style favored in some. *The
Mirror* is also notable because its authors were consciously col-
laborating, while the lyric miscellanies were usually gathered
without the consent of poets whose works were included.

The first Elizabethan miscellany, *A Handful of Pleasant
Delights,* was a clear descendant of Tottel's *Songes and Sonnettes.* Only one complete copy, dated 1584, survives, but Hyder
Rollins has verified as its first edition the *Very pleasaunte
Sonettes and storyes in myter* entered in the *Stationers' Register*
of 1566. Two existing fragments may be from the lost 1566
edition, or perhaps from others now unknown.[19] All the poems
are broadside ballads, all had previously been printed, and each
bears the name of its tune. Clement Robinson collected the
ballads and wrote some of them. The printer, Richard Jones,
continued his interest in miscellanies with the later *A Small*

Handful of Fragrant Flowers (1575), *A Gorgeous Gallery of Gallant Inventions* (1578), *Brittons Bowre of Delights* (1591), and *The Arbor of Amorous Devices* (1594). The title page of the *Handful* boasts the novelty of the poems—"Containing sundrie new Sonets and delectable Histories . . . Newly deuised to the newest tunes"—but both texts and tunes were already known.

The study of broadside ballads has become complex, and we can only suggest here their relationship to the chain of miscellanies.[20] The term includes any poetry printed on a broadside and intended for singing. The subjects were myriad: amorous, sentimental, or edifying; histories from the chronicles or romances from medieval gests. Some were journalistic rather than literary, reporting current marvels and the events of the day. Few of the great miscellanies lacked a poem that had appeared, or would later appear, on a broadside. For example, twelve poems in *Tottel's Miscellany* were soon registered for publication as ballads, and two were "moralized" into that form.[21] In other instances compilers of miscellanies drew upon broadsides already existing for part of their material. The broadsides, as a medium, were musical, popular, abundant, and readily accessible. There was a constant interaction of vitality and borrowing between them and the miscellanies.

Students of the ballads today disagree on the level of their audience and hence on their position as courtly or popular poetry. Ballads were roundly scorned by Elizabethan literary men. Jonson is typical in his attack on the "extemporall dinne of balladry" and in his firm distinction: "A poet should detest a ballad-maker."[22] Rollins himself sees the poems in the *Handful* as printed, not for the literary reader, but for the vulgar. As such, he sets the collection in "the greatest possible contrast to the miscellanies from *Tottel's* to *A Poetical Rhapsody* [1602], which were compiled for an altogether different group of readers."[23] But more plausible are the reservations of C. R. Baskervill, who demonstrates that ballads were in vogue among the courtly as well. Most literary men at the opening of Elizabeth's reign (Surrey, John Harington, John Heywood, George Gascoigne, Thomas Howell, George Turberville, Barnabe Googe) were writing ballads with classical stories or lovers' complaints. In subject, language, and conceits, the *Handful* ballads are similar to the poems of *Tottel's Miscellany,* the *Paradise,* and the *Gorgeous Gallery,* with their more aristocratic origins. Baskervill believes the divorce of the cultured from the ballad came later, as the result of the Puritan struggle.[24]

One implication of this controversy was the wide appeal of the early miscellanies and their poems. Their popularity was too fluid to allow any rigid division into courtly and vulgar. The first ballad in the *Handful,* "A Nosegaie alwaies sweet," gave Ophelia her gentle song of rosemary and violet, while the ballad of Pyramus and Thisbe may have provided Shakespeare's delightful burlesque in *A Midsummer Night's Dream.* There was matter (and treatment) both high and low in the ballads of Elizabeth's reign.

The *Handful* was literally that, with its thirty-two poems. Nearly all are about love, but there is charming diversity. Several are weighted with proverbs and homely saws; some turn classical tales into romantic tragedy; a few offer personal experience like George Mannington's lament "I wail in wo," most popular in the volume. The book has ingenuousness approaching the grace of plain style, and elsewhere shows the vitality of speaking voices, with the roughness of verses parted from their tunes. There is a version of "Greensleeves" and, directly in the middle (no. 16) like a surprising center of gravity, a ballad on "The Joys of Virginity." The *Handful* is an unpretentious volume and worthy of the modest promise of its title.

In 1575 Richard Jones issued a tiny book, ascribed to Nicholas Breton, which glanced at its predecessor's title: *A Small Handful of Fragrant Flowers.*[25] The poems were not entirely by Breton;

whether it was a true miscellany or not, it clearly sought connection with a successful one. Its few verses compare with flowers the virtues suitable for a gentlewoman, and embellish the lesson with Old Testament references.

In 1576 *The Paradise of Dainty Devices,* most popular of all the miscellanies, began its long career in print. Compiled by Richard Edwards, poet and playwright who died ten years before its publication, the volume went through ten known editions by 1606.[20] The first printing included 99 poems; after additions and subtractions, a total of 125 had been printed by the fourth extant edition, after which no more changes were made. The title page advertises a claim to gravity and courtly birth: "aptly furnished, with sundry pithie and learned inventions: devised and written for the most part, by M. Edwards, sometimes of her Maiesties Chappel: the rest, by sundry learned Gentlemen, both of honor, and woorshippe." The contributors included the best-known poets of the mid-century, and others about whom nothing is known. The Earl of Oxford, Lord Vaux, and Jasper Heywood (son of John Heywood, writer of proverbs and interludes) appear on the title page, among others, and Thomas Churchyard, William Hunnis, George Whetstone, and Francis Kinwelmarsh are included in the book. The first poem is a translation of *de contemptu mundi* verses by Saint Bernard, whose name heads the printed list of authors.

The *Paradise* has more variety of theme and tone than has previously been acknowledged, but it is basically sober and edifying. Saint Bernard's poem is a fitting introduction to the prevailing motifs that follow: the fickleness of fortune, the vanity of pleasures, laments for slander, feigned friends, sufferings in love. Like the other miscellanies this one has, at least in its early editions, a fair proportion of love poetry, but nearly all is complaint or warning. Some of the amorous verse was dropped in later editions, perhaps because it fared badly in comparison with the love poetry of the brilliant 1580s and 1590s. The moralizing verse in this collection weathered shifts of taste until the end of the century.

A highly wrought artificiality marks these poems designed to edify and admonish. A theme of this kind becomes relentless through figures of sound:

> I rage in restless ruthe, and ruins rule my daies,
> I rue (to late) my rechlesse youthe,
>   by rule of reasons waies:
> I ran so long a race, in searche of surest waie,
> That leasure learnde me tread the trace,
>   that led to leud decaie.

In this volume, as in the *Gorgeous Gallery,* many of the poems are top-heavy with rhetoric. The ingenuity of the figures, the repetitions to reinforce moral themes, overpower their subjects. Ultimately such use of language is homiletic, rather than poetic.

The *Paradise* also has a definite musical background, now largely inaccessible. Like most of the early miscellanies, it was meant to contain singing matter. Printer Henry Disle notes in his dedication that the "ditties . . . wyll yeelde a farre greater delight, being as they are so aptly made to be set to any song in 5 partes, or song to instrument." Twelve of the poems were either first published as ballads, or apparently were written to be sung as ballads, and Rollins notes the extant musical settings of several others. At least in text, these are the pieces favored by John Hall, who describes them as "Ryght sober songes godly and sadde."

The only miscellany having a direct resemblance to the *Greek Anthology* appeared the year after the *Paradise.* Timothe Kendall gathered *Flowers of Epigrams* (1577) from "as well auncient as late writers."[27] The first section prints epigrams from Martial, Ausonius, and other classical authors, along with those from Sir Thomas Elyot, Roger Ascham, Nicholas Grimald, Surrey, and other "moderns." Arranged by author, these are followed by a section of "Trifles" by Kendall himself, about a fourth of the book's total length. The subjects, seemingly chosen at random, include precepts and jests, definitions, epitaphs, and similitudes. Kendall's section adds an occasional polemic against the Roman church. There is little that is memorable in the translations and poems, but the volume shows a kinship with the classical anthology which one would expect to find somewhere in the history of the miscellanies. Greek studies flourished at the universities in the early sixteenth century, though it is doubtful that the *Greek Anthology* gave direct impetus to any other English collections.[28] But in Kendall's collection the native voice and the classical precedent meet. The result, it seems, had no further imitators.

Highly imitative, however, was the volume printed in 1578 by Richard Jones, who hoped to capitalize on the popularity of the *Paradise*. Jones's *A Gorgeous Gallery of Gallant Inventions* borrowed liberally from the *Handful,* from *Tottel's Miscellany,* and from the *Paradise,* as well as culling broadside ballads.[29] The title page declares the collection was "ioyned together and builded up: by T. P." (Thomas Proctor, who contributed some poems). Most of the verse is unsigned, but some contributors can be identified: Owen Roydon, Lord Vaux, Thomas Churchyard, Jasper Heywood, Thomas Howell, and Clement Robinson, who had compiled the *Handful* for Jones. The list is similar to that of the *Paradise,* although not so long; the *Gorgeous Gallery* introduced few new poets or inventions. The contents rely on moral commonplaces and conventional love situations, fraught with rhetorical energy as abundantly as the *Paradise* poems. Like some of the *Handful* ballads (some, of course, are borrowed), the verses display now a fine fervor, ingenuous despite their mannered style, and now a roughness that merely obscures feeling.

The *Gorgeous Gallery,* which evidently had no second edition, was seldom referred to by Elizabethan writers.[30] This fact is puzzling in view of the taste of the age and the steady persistence of the *Paradise* in public favor. Although the *Gallery* contains a higher proportion of amorous verse than its predecessor, it too has a moral earnestness that was growing old-fashioned by the 1570s. The poetry of amplified proverbs was disappearing. Readers continued to buy, but poets wrote no more of it. By the time the next important miscellanies appeared in the 1590s, the moral impulse was in a different mode, and the dialectic of moral and amorous verse was taking new forms.

Three volumes falling between the *Gallery* and *Brittons Bowre of Delights* (1591) deserve comment. *The Forrest of Fancy* (1579) is a slim book of forty-four poems mingled with twenty-one prose epistles. Its title page advertises diversity of form and a mixture of teaching and delight: "Wherein is conteined very prety Apothegmes, and pleasaunt histories, both in meeter and prose, Songes, Sonets, Epigrams and Epistles, of diuerse matter and in diuerse manner. With sundry other deuises, no lesse pithye then pleasaunt and profytable."[31] The only ascription anywhere is the initials H. C. at the end of the volume, which have been variously interpreted as Henry Cheke, Henry Constable, and Henry Chettle. J. P. Collier believed the book to be a miscellany edited by H. C.[32] The poetry often has the solemnity of admonition and warning—on the vanity of the world or the deceptions of women—but there is some levity in the epigrams.

In 1581 *Howell's Devises* appeared, primarily composed by Thomas Howell but with poems initialed by several other authors.[33] Like *The Forrest of Fancy*, this volume is slight both in size and in importance, and it is only technically a miscellany. To describe its poetry is basically to discuss Howell, gentleman-retainer to the Pembroke family and a minor link between the traditions of Surrey and Sidney. The book seems to mark the end of the direct influence of *Tottel's Miscellany*, although the indirect effects of that famous work are immeasurable. Howell's poems and those of his friends borrow themes and meters from

Tottel's collection. Their poulter's measure and fourteeners were archaic by 1581, as was their use of adages. Some of the poetry suggests musical accompaniment; there is a version of the ever present willow song, followed by another, ballad-like song, "All of greene Lawrell." Devices of sound—especially anaphora and alliteration—recur, but without the fervor reached in the *Paradise* and the *Gallery*. Howell's letter to the reader suggests a distrust of rhetorical artifice, but he invokes a guide claimed by poets of many persuasions:

> Where none but Nature is the guyde,
> > MINERVA hath no parte,
> Then you her Nurcelings beare with him,
> > yt knows no aide of arte.
>
> . . . .
> If patterns wrought by Arte,
> > of curious workman here thou seeke,
> Thy trauayle then thou shalt but lose,
> > to looke and neuer leeke
> But if good-will may thee suffise, peruse,
> > and take thy pleasure,
> In Natures schoole my little skill:
> > I learned all by leasure.

Although *Howell's Devises* reveals Petrarchan patterns and conceits that are basic to the love poetry of the 1590s, it looks backward to older motifs. One poem was probably borrowed from a dumb show in *Gorboduc,* one from a law court parable by Gascoigne, and two are dream visions, the first describing a banquet and the love court of Venus. Anticipating a later style of irony, one poem likens man's life to a stage play, and another argues that the golden age is not past but is here, since gold controls human actions. The acrostic use of a lady's name, as a courtly compliment, is carried over into *Brittons Bowre of Delights* and *The Arbor of Amorous Devices,* published in the 1590s.

The third volume to appear in the gap between the *Gallery*

and the volumes ascribed to Breton is *A Banquet of Dainty Conceits,* signed by A. M. (Anthony Munday) and printed in 1588.[14] Its title falls into the familiar vein of miscellany names; like *A Handful of Pleasant Delights,* it is made up entirely of ballads. Multiple authorship is possible but hard to determine. Whether or not the collection includes different poets, it is an interesting analogue to the very popular *Handful.* There is proportionately little on love, and many of the ballads contain moral reflections. The epistle to the reader assures him that the subject matter is "not fantasticall and full of love-quirkes and quiddities, yet stored with good admonitions and freendly documents." Also noteworthy is the assertion that the effectiveness of its poems depends on their tunes, which are named: some "will seeme very bad stuffe in reading, but (I perswade me) will delight thee, when thou singest any of them to thy instrument."

It seems remarkable that so few ballad collections are extant, since ballads were abundant and popular. Two volumes written mainly by Thomas Deloney (*The Garland of Good Will* [*SR* 1593] and *Strange Histories of Kings, Princes, Dukes,* . . . [1602]) are the only others known. However, ballads were freely printed and adapted in other miscellanies. The lowest broadside poetry remained on the so-called flying leaves, while the more sophisticated found a place in print with courtly or learned poetry.

CHAPTER II

THE LATER COLLECTIONS

T HERE WAS NOTABLE CHANGE in the two volumes printed by Richard Jones in the 1590s. *Brittons Bowre of Delights* (1591), a distinctly courtly anthology, is more exclusively amorous than any earlier one.[1] It includes several acrostic poems for court ladies, including Penelope Rich, and, of greatest interest, six poems in memory of Sidney. The printer's address "To the Gentlemen Readers" further suggests that the court is both the subject and the origin of the miscellany. Jones commends the poems "for the Subiet and worthinesse of the persons they doo concerne." The new pastoral interest probably reflects the influence of Sidney and his circle.

Most of the fifty-six poems in the first edition (forty-one in the 1597 edition) were written by Nicholas Breton, but Jones boldly used the name to identify the whole. Breton's opinion of this license appeared in his preface to *The Pilgrimage To Paradise, Ioyned With The Countesse of Penbrookes loue* (1592):

Gentlemen there hath beene of late printed in london by one Richarde Joanes, a printer, a booke of english verses, entituled *Bretons bower of delights:* I protest it was donne altogether without my consent or knowledge, and many thinges of other mens mingled with few of mine, for except *Amoris Lachrimae:* an epitaphe vpon Sir Phillip Sydney, and one or two other toies, which I know not how he vnhappily came by, I haue no part with any of them: and so I beseech yee assuredly beleeue.[2]

Nevertheless, Jones issued *The Arbor of Amorous Deuices* only two years later, in 1594, with a similar ascription, "By N. B., Gent.," although this time he admitted in his preface that it was "many mens workes excellent Poets, and most, not the meanest in estate and degree."

Although Jones did not boast the novelty of the poems in *Brittons Bowre,* he might well have. All but two were printed in the collection for the first time, two are found only there, and many others were never printed anywhere else, although they exist in manuscript. Some of the old bonds linking *A Handful of Pleasant Delights, The Paradise of Dainty Devices,* and *A Gorgeous Gallery of Gallant Inventions* seem to be broken, and the Breton volumes have a freshness unknown in the earlier, derivative volumes. *Brittons Bowre* prints one condensed version of a Surrey poem from *Tottel's Miscellany,* suggesting descent from that volume. In terms of borrowings, however, *Brittons Bowre* is oriented toward the future: ten of its poems were reprinted in *The Arbor of Amorous Devices* and four in *England's Helicon* (1600).

The moral earnestness of collections from the 1570s is entirely gone now, and conventions of love and pastoral prevail. The volume opens with Breton's lament for Sidney, "Amoris Lachrimae," in sixty-one stanzas. Sidney is likened to the phoenix, mourned by allegorical figures of Love, Art, and Beauty, lamented by shepherds whose Pan has broken his pipes, and by Nature who responds by withering. The familiar artifices of pastoral elegy are here, and the rest of the book is in thematic harmony. Five other short epitaphs on Sidney, scattered through the volume, address a presence that is evident in the whole. The pastoral verse of *Brittons Bowre,* almost unknown in earlier miscellanies, is emerging toward the chaste and lyrical simplicity that distinguishes *England's Helicon.* Lines like the following strike the ear as a promise:

> Good Muse rocke me asleepe with some sweet harmonie,
>   This weary eie is not to keepe, thy warie companie.
> Sweet Loue be gone a while, thou knowst my heauines,
>   Bewtie is borne but to beguile my heart of happiness.

Alliteration and poulter's measure, which had a near stranglehold on earlier poetry, are here handled with moderation and grace. Twenty years before, no one could tame that intractable meter to a musical line.

Yet despite this foreshadowing of a new lyricism, *Brittons Bowre* has its old-fashioned elements. It includes five dream poems, probably all by Breton, and one complaint begins with a stanza of disembodied maxims. Breton's originality at some points is matched by his fondness for anaphora and other mechanical devices of ordering. So the volume is not a reversal of old patterns, but rather a significant turn toward new forms.

In many respects *The Arbor of Amorous Devices* (1594) is a companion piece to *Brittons Bowre*.[8] Its forty-four poems include acrostic tributes, two pieces from *Tottel's Miscellany*, several dream poems, and the prevailing pastoral and love conceits. There are no poems to Sidney, but one by him, from the *Arcadia,* is included. Midway in the collection is Breton's long poem on the love of God surpassing other love, but it is only a graceful diversion in a volume promising on its title page that "young Gentlemen may reade many plesant fancies, and fine deuises: And thereon, meditate diuers sweete Conceites, to court the loue of faire Ladies and Gentle-women." Thirty of the poems had not appeared elsewhere in print before 1592. But Jones needed to reprint the last ten poems from *Brittons Bowre* to fill out his book, and he had lost some poems to a rival compiler: "and had not the Phenix preuented me of some the best stuffe she furnisht her nest with of late: this *Arbor* had bin somewhat the more handsomer trimmed vp" (from the preface to readers). The popularity of the two "Breton" volumes is shown by the frequent reprinting of their verses, and by their reappearance in numerous manuscript commonplace books.

The public interest in miscellanies may have been responsible for the inclusion of thirty-five poems by "sundrie other Noblemen and Gentlemen" in the pirated 1591 edition of

Sidney's *Astrophel and Stella*.⁴ Twenty-eight of Samuel Daniel's sonnets appear here, as well as poems by Thomas Campion and Fulke Greville. The corrected second quarto (1591) lacks the "others," but a final quarto (1597?) reprints them. The publisher of the first, Thomas Newman, was following common practice in making free with poems he thought valuable. Apparently he also felt that a miscellaneous volume would have special appeal to buyers.

The next genuine miscellany was *The Phoenix Nest* (1593) which had so aroused Richard Jones's envy.⁵ One of the most beautiful of the collections, it printed a wider range of impressive poets than had any earlier volume. No authors' names are given for its seventy-eight poems, and only a third of the pieces are discreetly initialed. Ranging from certain to likely are the identifications of Thomas Lodge, Breton, the Earl of Oxford, Sir Edward Dyer, George Peele, Robert Greene, Thomas Watson, Raleigh, and Greville. Still in doubt is the identity of the "R. S. of the Inner Temple, Gentleman," who compiled the volume, "Built vp with the most rare and refined workes of Noble men, woorthy Knights, gallant Gentlemen, Masters of Arts, and braue Schollers." *The Phoenix Nest* was apparently the only miscellany, except for *A Poetical Rhapsody* (1602), to be collected under the supervision of a gentleman rather than a printer. The acquaintance and taste of this gentleman-amateur account for the omission of poets one might expect to find in a 1593 miscellany. Michael Drayton, Spenser, Sidney, Marlowe, and Shakespeare appeared in *England's Helicon* seven years later, but not in *The Phoenix Nest*. Nevertheless, R. S. was a skillful editor, providing in Rollins's view "the most carefully printed miscellany, one of the most carefully printed books, of the period."⁶

The volume opens with a prose defense of the Earl of Leicester, followed by three elegies for Sidney. The rest of the first half is in medieval modes, but with contemporary stylistic features: a poem praising chastity, two dream poems, an allegorized chess game, and several others. A section of love poems, more typical of the 1590s, concludes the volume. The inclusion of fifteen sonnets gives more emphasis to this verse form than any miscellany since Tottel's, although the term had been used with its wider meaning in many collections. The sonneteering vogue was at its height in 1593 and is fairly reflected in *The Phoenix Nest*. Many of the love poems, perhaps even a majority, are drawn from French and Italian models, especially from Pierre de Ronsard and Phillipe Desportes. Although this feature also links the book with *Tottel's Miscellany,* the fashion for foreign borrowings was simply recurring; the element is not a sign of old-fashioned taste.

Surprisingly, *The Phoenix Nest* had no known second edition, although its poems reappeared in manuscripts and several were reprinted in *England's Helicon* and *A Poetical Rhapsody.* The outburst of poetry, sonnets and other verse forms, in the 1590s was more formidable competition than earlier miscellanies had met.

Many of the light-handed editorial methods of the time were illustrated by William Jaggard, who printed *The Passionate Pilgrim* in 1599.[7] He ascribed the small volume entirely to Shakespeare, although only five of its twenty poems are his, and he had evidently sought out Shakespeare's "private" poems mentioned by Francis Meres a year earlier in his *Palladis Tamia.* The last six poems have a separate title page: "Sonnets to sundry notes of Musicke." Sir Sidney Lee suggests that all six had been set by contemporary composers and that a lost edition might have supplied the music.[8] The volume was twice reprinted, the third edition (1612) being much enlarged by the addition of Thomas Heywood's translation of two Ovidian epistles.[9]

Shakespeare's sonnets 138 and 144 were first printed in *The Passionate Pilgrim,* along with three poems from *Love's La-*

bour's Lost. The remaining poems are by Richard Barnfield, Bartholomew Griffin, Marlowe, and others whose identity is less certain. Five of these are in the six-line stanzas of Shakespeare's *Venus and Adonis,* a form common in most of the miscellanies since *The Paradise of Dainty Devices.* Four sonnets are on the theme of Venus and Adonis. Jaggard probably meant thus to link the volume even more closely to Shakespeare's name, for the 1612 edition adds the subtitle, "or Certaine Amorous Sonnets betweene Venus and Adonis." The poems are all about love, with pleasingly varied inventions. Marlowe's "Come live with me and be my love," later reappearing in *England's Helicon,* is here with one stanza of the probable answer by Raleigh. Barnfield's sonnet, praising John Dowland and Edmund Spenser, presses a love suit on grounds "If Musicke and sweet Poetrie agree." The pastoral world and its pathetic fallacy form the setting for some of the other lyrics. The tiny volume frankly mixed erotic verse with a background of madrigals and capitalized upon Shakespeare's name for a considerable popularity.

The next year the most beautiful and distinguished of all the miscellanies was published. *England's Helicon* (1600) gathers at the end of the century the most charming lyrics from the past two decades.[10] The collection is entirely pastoral, although the editor freely altered poems to reflect that convention. Of the total of 159 poems, many have new titles, speakers, or lines adapting them to the pastoral mode. Still there is enough diversity of form and of individual talent to enliven the volume; the organic principle unifies as well as restricts. It is now agreed that Nicholas Ling edited the work under the patronage of John Bodenham, although Bodenham was long assigned the book in library catalogues. He was a notable collector and compiler, responsible for a series of quotation books, including *Belvedere* (1600) and the prose *Politeuphuia: Wits Common wealth* (1597) and *Wits Theater of the Little World* (1599).[11] *England's Helicon* is prefaced by a sonnet from A. B. to "his loving kinde friend" Bodenham commending the latter's "designe" of the collections.

England's Helicon shows the widest background of any miscellany. Its compiler drew two poems from Tottel's *Songes and Sonnettes* and six from *The Phoenix Nest.* Others came from Sidney's *Astrophel and Stella,* Watson's *Hecatompathia,* Michael Drayton's *Idea,* Lodge's *Phillis,* and Spenser's *Shepherd's Calendar* and *Astrophel.* There are songs from plays and romances: from Lodge's *Rosalind,* Sidney's *Arcadia,* Greene's *Menaphon,* Peele's *Arraignement of Paris,* Shakespeare's *Love's Labour's Lost.* Lyrics were taken from madrigal collections and songbooks of the day, and certain poems by Henry Constable, Anthony Munday, and Bartholomew Yong appear for the first time. A total of thirty authors are indicated, by name or initials, with a number of poems signed "Anonymous" or "Ignoto." Conjectures about authorship have proceeded apace. An interesting but misleading contemporary list of *Helicon* poems and authors is in the handwriting of Francis Davison, compiler of *A Poetical Rhapsody* in 1602.[12] Davison avoided repeating any of the *Helicon* poems in his own collection, but his ascriptions in the list are not to be trusted.

Since more than three-fourths of the poems in the first edition of *England's Helicon* had already appeared in print, the publisher could not—and did not—make the claim for novelty found in some earlier volumes. The *Helicon* has a sureness of literary taste which makes publisher's puffs unnecessary. Only the tedious and wooden lines of Bartholomew Yong, in twenty-five selections, have consistently been called flaws in the volume. But even these poems have been spaced in some evident concern for structure.

Like *The Passionate Pilgrim,* the *Helicon* is entirely amorous, although the pastoral convention allows for moral reflection in the terms of a pastoral world. The old poems of admonition

and adage are long since gone; the pastoral metaphor finds
out its moral directions by indirection. The single shepherd's
complaint from Tottel is reprinted here, some forty years later,
in the fair company of a fully developed convention. The
closeness to music prized in the early miscellanies is still vital;
in *England's Helicon* poetic language not only is set to music,
but is itself musical in new ways.

By the end of the century didactic poetry was also completing
an evolution. The amplified maxims popular in *Tottel's Miscellany* and *The Paradise of Dainty Devices* had lost their
rhetorical elaborations and were returning to printed sententiae.
Bodenham's *Belvedere or The Garden of the Muses* (1600) is
a dictionary of quotations, rather than a true miscellany, and
all its passages are limited to one or two lines each.[13] But it
is a clear descendant of earlier didactic verse, purged of the
figuration now more judiciously employed in love poetry. The
preface to the reader describes the "garden": the flowers are
"most learned, graue, and wittie sentences," including "store
of hearbs to heale" and "flowres of comfort." None of the
quotations is signed, but the compiler lists as contributors some
forty of the best-known poets of the time. Among the most
frequently cited were Shakespeare, Spenser, Marlowe, and
Daniel. The collection is divided by *topoi*—God, heaven, con-
science, war, fame, age, and so on—with three subdivisions in
each category: definitions, similes, and examples. A modern
reader doubts whether to call the volume poetry, and it does
have some prose quotations simply rendered in lines. But other
influences lie behind its aphoristic purpose.

Several precedents for the dictionaries of quotations had
achieved wide popularity earlier in the century. After the manner of Erasmus's proverbs, Sir Thomas Elyot translated wise
sayings from the ancients in *The Bankette of Sapience* (1539).[14]
Four editions of his book, arranged with headings similar to
those in *Belvedere,* had appeared by 1564. More complex in

structure and immensely popular was *The Treatise of Moral Philosophy containing the Sayings of the Wise* (1547) by William Baldwin, who had been largely responsible for *A Mirror for Magistrates.*[15] Two-thirds of Baldwin's book is made up of precepts and proverbs, arranged by theme and also drawn from classical wisdom. The book was in print continuously for nearly a hundred years, having eighteen editions by 1640. All these works were in prose, but they are closely related to Bodenham's *Belvedere* and to the four prose parts of *Wits Common wealth,* in which Bodenham had a guiding interest. *Politeuphuia* and *Wits Theater* have been mentioned above: *Palladis Tamia: Wits Treasury Being the Second part of Wits Common wealth* by Francis Meres (1598) and *Palladis Palatium: Wisedoms Pallace or The fourth part of Wits Common wealth* (1604) complete the series. Reversing the occasional tranformations in *Belvedere, Politeuphuia* has some verse quotations made into prose. Obviously, this family of volumes strays only incidentally into the tradition of poetical miscellanies.

Closer to the lyric collections is another "dictionary" published in 1600, *England's Parnassus,* compiled by Robert Allot.[16] A long work with 2,350 passages, it shows a different emphasis in its subtitle: "The choysest Flowers of our Moderne Poets, with their Poeticall comparisons. Descriptions of Bewties, Personages Castles, Palaces, Mountaines, Groues, Seas, Springs, Riuers, &C." Like the other books of the same type, it begins with quotations by topic, then adds sections with richly imaged descriptions of beauties, natural and poetic. Some passages are brief, but other run as long as forty lines. Aphorism is clearly less valued than poetic invention in this apparent handbook for imitation. All the quotations are signed, but with much inaccuracy, and the book has been a mixed blessing to bibliographers. But it clearly includes pieces from the most important poets and playwrights of the day. Sidney Lee finds here "one of the most convincing pieces of contemporary testimony to the

popularity of Shakespeare's work in the early part of his career."[17] Like all the miscellanies, *England's Parnassus* is a sure
index to the repute of poets at its date, allowing always for the
taste and the acquaintanceship of the compiler.

A Shakespearean interest also attaches to Robert Chester's
Love's Martyr or Rosalins Complaint (1601).[18] It is not a true
anthology, but a long, curious allegorical poem of Chester's
followed by a shorter section of "Diverse Poeticall Essaies on
the Turtle and Phoenix." These short poems celebrating the
phoenix theme are by Shakespeare, George Chapman, John
Marston, Ben Jonson, and perhaps others. The figures in the
first poem, said to be "Allegorically shadowing the truth of
Loue, in the constant Fate of the Phoenix and Turtle," have
been variously interpreted. Grosart believed the two to be
Elizabeth and Essex, while others have found connections with
Sir John Salisbury, to whom the poem is dedicated.[19] The short
poems, almost equally cryptic, depend for their interpretation
upon the uncertain significance of Chester's allegory. The volume has no near relatives among the verse collections, although
the phoenix appears incidentally in several others, and some
volumes celebrate court persons in mildly riddling forms. The
hint of political overtones in Chester's poem, along with mention of "the annuals of great Brittaine" and "the true legend
of famous King Arthur," is oddly reminiscent of *The Faerie
Queene*. The distinction of the poets, although not of the poetry, has maintained some interest in the book, but it remains
an anomaly among the poetical miscellanies.

Two ballad collections drawn up in the last decade of Elizabeth's reign must be mentioned here. Both were principally
by Thomas Deloney, although both have traditional material
only partly shaped by him, and there are ballads by other
writers. *The Garland of Good Will* was entered in the *Stationers'
Register* in 1593, although the earliest extant copy is dated 1631.[20]
Many of the twenty-seven ballads in this edition had been reg-

istered separately as broadsides. Their diversity suggests nearly the full range of subject matter found in ballads at the end of the century: pastoral dialogue, historical subjects like Lady Rosamond, complaints of love, patriotic praise of the English rose, a dialogue between Truth and Ignorance in the manner of a medieval *débat*. Many of the ballads are narrative, drawn from the chronicles, and names of tunes are given for many of the verses.

The second volume, printed in 1602, recalls *A Mirror for Magistrates* in historical and moral emphasis. Its title is indicative: *Strange Histories of Kings, Princes, Dukes, Earles, Lords, Ladies, Knights, and Gentlemen . . . a most excellent warning for all estates.*[21] There are only ten ballads, each prefixed by a line or two of music. They cover a fairly wide range of historical material, including a battle with William the Conqueror, the death of Edward II, and Wat Tyler's Rebellion. The modern editor suggests that the ballads probably had not circulated before, since all are versified from Holinshed's *Chronicle* and arranged chronologically. The ballad stanzas set the volume apart from the *Mirror,* but a similar didactic gravity is urged from the lessons of history.

A fitting conclusion to the history of Elizabethan miscellanies is Francis Davison's *A Poetical Rhapsody,* first printed in 1602. This collection reached a fourth edition by 1621, by which time it included a total of 250 poems, making it the longest miscellany except for Tottel's. The arrangement was substantially changed in each new edition, probably to give the appearance of an entirely new book. The familiar claim of the first title page, that its verse was "Neuer yet published," was largely true. Its nineteenth-century editor, A. H. Bullen, believed it "in some respects . . . the most valuable of our old anthologies" because it was "in great part compiled from unpublished writings." Its destruction would thus have meant "the irretrievable loss of much excellent poetry."[22]

Francis Davison, son of a secretary to the Queen, was a young man when he edited *A Poetical Rhapsody*. He and his younger brother Walter, who "was not 18. yeeres olde when hee writt these Toyes" (says the preface to the reader), contributed a section of poems ascribed to them; a total of eighty-two in all the editions were assigned to Francis, and nineteen to Walter. Following this section in the first printing is a group of sixty-nine poems headed by the puzzling name Anomos, whom Davison calls his "deere friend." There are about fifty other poems, some in an introductory group, the rest in a final section. Of these additions, Davison says "the mixing (both at the beginning and ende of this booke) of diuerse thinges written by great and learned Personages, with our meane and worthles Scriblings, I vtterly disclaime it, as being done by the Printer." Thus it is hard to determine responsibility for the content and the structure of the book; Davison clearly had no hand in any edition beyond the second, if indeed in that. The added sections include lyrics by a wide range of poets, some of them signed: Raleigh, Spenser, Sidney, the Countess of Pembroke, Watson, Greene, Campion, Henry Constable, and others.

The diversity of styles and types in *A Poetical Rhapsody* is nearly unrivaled in other miscellanies. The title page of the second edition illustrates the variety: "Containing: Diuerse Sonnets, Odes, Elegies, Madrigals, Epigrams, Pastorals, Eglogues, with other Poems, both in Rime and Measured Verse." The contributions to the first edition are drawn from the work of approximately twenty-five years, and newly written poems were added to later printings. As a result, there are both anachronistic and current elements in each edition. The pastorals by Sidney and Spenser, and others indebted to them, seem old-fashioned for the seventeenth century, especially where archaic diction is used in deliberate imitation of Spenser. There are sonnets of many different schemes, late experimentation in that form now past its vogue. Like *Tottel's Miscellany,* the

Rhapsody depends notably on French and Italian models, including adaptations of Serafino, Petrarch, Clément Marot, and Luigi Groto. Davison had traveled extensively in France and Italy and, like Wyatt many decades before, had added the cosmopolitan to the native voice in his miscellany. There are a dozen poems in quantitative verse—hexameters, phaleuciacs, sapphics, and others—which also belong to an earlier short-lived taste. The numerous translations from the classics are neither old nor new, although no miscellany since *Flowers of Epigrams* had gathered so many. Anacreon, the *Greek Anthology,* Ovid, Martial, Horace—all are represented here. Finally, in the 1611 edition, two thirteenth-century Latin verses are included from the *De Contemptu Mundi* of John of Garland, followed by translations. The somber medieval note is arresting at this distance; it recalls the opening poem from Saint Bernard in *The Paradise of Dainty Devices.* The survival of such a voice, however brief, links *A Poetical Rhapsody* with its ancestry in *Songes and Sonnettes* and beyond.

A Poetical Rhapsody, however, was contemporary as well as reminiscent. The epigrammatic quatrains reflect a taste for brevity and wit, surpassing the earlier lame translations by Timothe Kendall. Some of the abundant madrigals and airs were taken from the most popular music books, and many were later reprinted in songbooks. The Petrarchan conventions still have their hold on much of the love poetry, but a recurring ironic edge anticipates the Cavalier spirit. The *Rhapsody* shows a varying array of poetic interests at the close of the century. It is noteworthy that this valuable work should be the last of the Elizabethan miscellanies, and the last of its like for many years to come.

The seventeenth century had few anthologies of lyric poetry. The Case bibliography of English poetical miscellanies, extending to 1750, records the majority of its entries between 1660 and 1750, but there were none like *England's Helicon* and *A*

Poetical Rhapsody. Case lists many volumes of classical translations and of polemics on state affairs. Collections of political
satire were especially common after the Restoration, and John
Dryden was adviser for a series of miscellanies published by
Jacob Tonson from 1684. But the best lyrical poets—George
Herbert, Henry Vaughan, Richard Crashaw, Robert Herrick,
and their contemporaries—were not used by anthologists until
the nineteenth century. The Elizabethan volumes traced in
these chapters were not reprinted after the 1621 edition of *A
Poetical Rhapsody* (except for the two ballad collections by
Deloney), until many of them were rediscovered by nineteenth-
century editors.

The Elizabethan miscellanies, abundant and popular, were
a considerable presence throughout the period. The first and
last of them nearly coincided in publication with the dates of
Elizabeth's reign: 1557 and 1602. Except for *The Court of
Venus,* the form belonged only to that reign, in which it developed, flourished, became diversified, and then disappeared.
The collections recorded persistent moral concerns and a medieval inheritance, but they also looked forward to the emerging
lyric voice of the late century. Many took shape or substance
from poetic conventions; of these, four volumes may serve as
landmarks in the developing history of the form.

CHAPTER III

TOTTEL'S MISCELLANY: A SOURCE
BOOK FOR ELOQUENCE

OTTEL'S MISCELLANY has long been the best known of the Elizabethan collections. Its claim is historical: until Russell Fraser's work on *The Court of Venus,* leading to his 1955 edition of the fragments, Tottel's collection was thought to be the first printed anthology.

Tottel himself had a more specific intention for his book than has been generally recognized; he explains his purpose in his preface to the reader:

That to have wel written in verse, yea & in small parcelles, deserveth great praise, the workes of divers Latines, Italians, and other, doe prove sufficiently. That our tong is able in that kynde to do as praiseworthely as the rest, the honorable stile of the noble earle of Surrey, and the weightinesse of the depewitted sir Thomas Wyat the elders verse, with severall graces in sondry good Englishe writers, doe show abundantly. It resteth nowe (gentle reder) that thou thinke it not evill doon, to publish, to the honor of the Englishe tong, and for profit of the studious of Englishe eloquence, those workes which the ungentle horders up of such treasure have heretofore envied thee. . . . If parhappes some mislike the statelinesse of stile removed from the rude skill of common eares: I aske help of the learned to defend their learned frendes, the authors of this work: And I exhort the unlearned, by reding to learne to be more skilfull, and to purge that swinelike grossenesse, that maketh the swete maierome [marjoram] not to smell to their delight.[1]

Tottel's Miscellany was intended to vindicate the English language, to exemplify and instruct in refinements of style. Except for the "weightinesse" of "depewitted" Wyatt's poems, there is no mention here of theme or content; there are none of the claims to pithiness, novelty, or diversity which crowd prefaces in later miscellanies. The concern is for eloquence of an

aristocratic kind: the "honorable stile" of Surrey, and a "statelinesse" belonging to "learned" authors. The final reproof of
rude, common readers seems calculated to mortify any de-
tractors before they might speak. The whole statement is an
amplified dedication: "to the honor of the Englishe tong."

Tottel's Miscellany became a source book for eloquence in
two ways. It made accessible a variety of poets and poetic types
in a book that was widely read and whose contents were often
imitated. And, always excepting that uncertain quantity, *The
Court of Venus,* it introduced the miscellany itself as a form.
In a result Tottel may not have intended or foreseen, the anthology became a model for future collections.

This second result has been little discussed, although modern scholars have generally agreed on Tottel's success in achieving the first. Two recent studies follow particular innovations
in the book, showing their transmission to following decades.
Vere L. Rubel discusses the new diction, modeled on Chaucer,
which here replaces the aureate language of John Skelton and
Stephen Hawes. Wyatt's conscious archaisms, followed in kind
by Surrey and the other Tottel poets, were a decided shift from
the unnatural borrowings of earlier poetry.[2] Archaisms, of
course, can themselves become an affectation, and these problems of language continued to be debated throughout the century. *Tottel's Miscellany,* however, confirmed the powers of
English as a language capable in itself of variety and refinement. Rubel also traces two other tendencies in this volume:
disarranged syntax to set off the diction of poetry from that
of ordinary communication, and reliance on verbal figures.

The second technical study is John Thompson's *The Founding of English Metre.* Admitting the regularizing changes made
by Tottel's editor, Thompson claims that Surrey's poulter's
measure had a strong influence on later poets. The blank verse
and the sonnets in the miscellany, as forms, were largely ignored for many years, but poulter's measure dominated English

poetry for twenty years after 1557.[3] In fact, with the conservatism already observed in many anthologies, seven poems in this meter appeared as late as 1591, in *Brittons Bowre of Delights*. C. S. Lewis also finds the primary importance of the Tottel poets in their meters: their main function was "to build a firm metrical highway out of the late medieval swamp," though "in Tottel we can discover traces of one or two uncompleted highways, systems of metre that were never worked out."[4]

Other critics, however, have read *Tottel's Miscellany* as a negative influence, or as a source book that ultimately worked against eloquence. H. A. Mason, concerned with early Tudor humanism, asks this question about the collection: "To what extent and in what spirit did the poets flourishing in and before 1550 continue the work of the times, that of transmuting the needed vitality from the Classics into vigorous native English?" He answers that the volume "marked a downward turn to sterility, and, though the first in time of the series of anthologies that became such a feature of the second half of the century, it is in fact the grave of Early Tudor poetry." "Everything,'" he believes, "had virtually to be done all over again in poetry. The poets who owe anything to the verse of Tottel's anthology constitute the backwater of the Elizabethan-Jacobean stream."[5]

Raymond Southall also blames the editor of *Tottel's Miscellany* for transmitting a debased form of early Tudor poetry. He finds in it "a weakening of contact with a range of attitudes and beliefs that, associated with notions of chivalry and courtly love, gives court poetry an extended connotation that stretches backwards over at least three centuries."[6] For Southall the decline of courtly love poetry was a betrayal of eloquence.

Douglas Peterson argues that the miscellany is no source book, at least for innovations. He claims that most of the lyrics are actually medieval in conception and technique, using rhetorical patterns from medieval handbooks.[7]

Nevertheless, praise from Elizabethan readers still validates

the success of Tottel's plan in his own century. Rollins, who believed the book was "largely responsible" for the great outburst
of Elizabethan lyricism, traces just a sample of the many allusions to it in the period. The volume was early a handbook for
such followers as Thomas Sackville, Barnabe Googe, and
George Turberville. In 1589 it was a practical source for George
Puttenham, who took dozens of quotations to illustrate rhetorical figures and called Wyatt and Surrey "the two chief lanternes
of light to all others that have since employed their pennes upon
English Poesie." His commendation of their poetry is in Tottel's
own terms:

In the later end of Henry VIII's raigne sprong up a new company
of courtly makers, of whom Sir Thomas Wyat th'elder and Henry
Earle of Surrey were the two chieftaines, who having travailed into
Italie, and there tasted the sweete and stately measures and stile of
the Italian Poesie . . . they greatly pollished our rude & homely maner
of vulgar Poesie, from that it had bene before, and for that cause may
justly be sayd the first reformers of our English meetre and stile.[8]

Still later, Jonson concurred in his *Discoveries* that Wyatt
and Surrey were "for their times admirable: and the more, because they began Eloquence with us."[9] Since the poets in *Tottel's
Miscellany* were known almost entirely from its pages, the
credit for their later influence—favorable or not—belongs to
Tottel's volume. Shakespeare himself showed his familiarity
with it at two points, and it was being read well beyond its last
known reprinting in 1587.[10]

The notion of eloquence governing this book depended
largely upon its editor, a figure still surrounded by many questions. Arber and many later scholars accepted Nicholas Grimald
as the editor, and perhaps even the compiler, of all the poems.
Rollins holds it "a reasonable and safe assumption," however,
that Tottel himself edited the first three printings of the miscellany.[11] Probably the poems were privately gathered into a commonplace book, from what scattered origins we can only guess,

and then this manuscript passed into Tottel's hands. Some of the editing may have been done before Tottel saw the collection. Certainly poetical manuscripts of the time were often marked with alternate readings, and copyists may have introduced changes through inaccuracy or their own "improvements." But Tottel himself or his agent probably set the prevailing aim of regularity for the poems.

To achieve this goal the texts were changed in various ways. Rough lines were altered into regular iambic movement. Words or phrases were inserted or omitted; phrases or even whole lines were sometimes transposed. Refrains were omitted in several of Wyatt's poems, and three of his rondeaux were changed into fourteen-line poems resembling sonnets. Besides these well-known changes in meter, the editor also substituted contemporary words for some archaic ones, occasionally eliminated end rhymes, censored references that were thought imprudent in the year 1557, and added titles to the poems. Today such alterations may be regarded as tampering, though Rollins accepts them as a "modernizing process" in which the editor brought his old-fashioned manuscript texts up to contemporary standards. Rollins maintains that the popularity of *Tottel's Miscellany,* and the reputation of its poets, were all the better for the editorial emendations.[12]

The refining of individual poems was apparently more important to the editor than was the structure of his anthology. He evidently gave little thought to progression or shape in the volume as a whole, an indifference shared by the compilers of most later miscellanies. The book is arranged according to poets, with four sections given, respectively, to Surrey, Wyatt, Grimald, and a group called the "uncertain authors." There are forty poems by Surrey, ninety-seven by Wyatt, forty by Grimald, and ninety-four by the anonymous group. In the second edition, which came out barely two months after the first, thirty of Grimald's poems had been dropped and his name reduced to initials, and the remaining ten had been moved to the end of the volume; thirty-nine poems by uncertain authors had been added; and several poems had been moved to follow others they answered or to join the sections by Surrey and Wyatt. In editions later than the second, the contents and their order remained the same.

Although the sections themselves have some structural ordering, the editor's main purpose was apparently to present his noted authors. Surrey appears first probably because, since he was the best-known contributor and was an aristocrat, his name promised an appeal for the volume. His section contains nearly all the short poems he wrote (apart from the biblical paraphrases and the *Aeneid* translations). The modern edition of his work prints only seven others.[13] This representation contrasts with Wyatt's, since Tottel included only about a third of the 268 poems now believed to be his.[14]

Nos. 1–25 in Surrey's section are love poetry, predominantly complaints with a very few poems of pledge or warning to the lover. No. 15 is his much admired reminiscence from Windsor prison. Nos. 6–14, forming a cluster of sonnets, lack thematic sequence but are clearly grouped together. The rest of the section has epigrammatic poems, on contentment and the "meane estate," and four elegies for Wyatt.

In Tottel's arrangement, Surrey's work introduces the "statelinesse of stile removed from the rude skill of common eares." Surrey's metrical principles were apparently close to those of Tottel's editor, who preferred regularity and even stresses. Nevertheless, the same regularizing tactics were used on his work as on Wyatt's, to a smaller degree. Only two of Surrey's poems survive in manuscripts dated earlier than Tottel's collection, and even the later manuscripts probably have corruptions, so that Surrey's exact texts will always be uncertain. It is safe to say, however, that his "honorable stile," with only minor changes, satisfied Tottel's ear.[15]

Surrey's meters and stanza forms are quite varied. This diversity, shared by the other sections, served well in a source book offered for study and imitation. There are stanzas of four, six, and seven lines, and the first poem in the book is a creditable example of terza rima. Its opening lines are almost perfectly iambic, showing Surrey's customary smoothness as clearly as anywhere:

> The sonne hath twise brought furth his tender grene,
> And clad the earth in liuely lustinesse:
> Ones haue the windes the trees despoiled clene,
> And new again begins their cruelnesse,
> The sonne hath twise brought furth his tender grene,
> Since I haue hid vnder my brest the harm
> That neuer shall recouer healthfulnesse.
> The winters hurt recouers with the warm:
> The parched grene restored is with shade.

Despite their regularity these lines are supple. The few nuances in the meter are enough to prevent rigidity.

A later poem shows even better the sweep and "statelinesse" that Surrey could achieve in basically iambic lines. His no. 29 praises Wyatt's Psalm translations:

> The great Macedon, that out of Persie chased
> Darius, of whose huge power all Asie rong,
> In the rich ark dan Homers rimes he placed,
> Who fayned gestes of heathen princes song.
> What holy graue? what worthy sepulture
> To Wiattes Psalmes should Christians then purchase?

There is little sign here of the restraining editorial hand. Even the end stopping common in all the poetry of this book is broken down, and a broader phrasing results.

Nine of Surrey's poems are in poulter's measure, a meter universally disliked today. Two problems always dog this measure. First, its six- and seven-foot lines are so long that they often require filling out, either with reiteration or with empty phrases.

Thus sense is subject to a rigid form and often fares the worse. Second, the caesura in each line enforces a fatal thumping effect, compounded by repetition in successive lines. Even when the sense of a line resists the pause, the meter demands it. Surrey's no. 19 opens:

Good Ladies, ye that haue your pleasures in exile,
  Step in your foote, come take a place & moorne with me a while.

The unwanted pause in the first line was sometimes emphasized by punctuation in later examples, as in "The yong man eke that feles, his bones with paines opprest." The filling out of Surrey's second line is obvious.

In one poem, however, Surrey shows his flexibility in stanzas based on fourteeners, couplets closely related to poulter's measure. The fourteeners are broken into four short lines, then amplified into longer ones:

When other louers in armes acrosse,
Reioyce their chiefe delight:
Drowned in teares to mourne my losse,
I stand the bitter night,
In my window, where I may see,
Before the windes how the cloudes flee.
Lo, what a mariner loue hath made me.

These lines have been much quoted and deserve the recognition. Delicacy of phrasing supersedes the demands of meter.

Besides his metrical variety, Surrey also offered examples of careful poetic structure. No. 31, longest of his poems on Wyatt ("W[yatt] resteth here, that quick could never rest"), praises the man by his parts—head, hand, tongue, and more. For the length of the poem, this catalogue arrangement is effective, and the final lines record the final division of the man:

Thus, for our gilte, this iewel have we lost:
The earth his bones, the heavens possesse his gost.[16]

Surrey's translation from Martial, on "The meanes to attain

happy life" (no. 27), underlines the structure of the original with tight parallel phrases and spareness of diction.

Most interesting to a modern reader are still Surrey's sonnets, which often combine metrical and structural skill. Eleven of his fifteen sonnets are Shakespearean in form; the others have fewer rhymes. But all have couplets, as do all of Wyatt's in this miscellany. Many of the sonnets are translated or adapted from Petrarch, so their structure is not strictly Surrey's own, but the balance of lines and the use of parallel constructions are often his. In no. 12, for example, "Set me whereas the sunne doth parche the grene," the units of sense are the quatrains, broadened from the original where every second line reiterates "Pommi . . . [Set me]." Surrey's first quatrain has four unbroken lines, while the second shifts to parallel lines parted by a caesura:

> Set me in hye, or yet in lowe degree:
> In longest night, or in the shortest daye:
> In clearest skye, or where clowdes thickest be:
> In lusty youth, or when my heeres are graye.

Typically, the versification is smooth and basically regular.

No. 2—"The soote season, that bud and blome furth brings"— is also characteristic. It uses the couplet for a rather facile contrast of the poet and nature. A play on words closes the irony:

> And thus I see among these pleasant thinges
> Eche care decayes, and yet my sorow springes.

Most important for imitators was the alliteration in lines like these:

> The adder all her sloughe awaye she slinges:
> The swift swalow pursueth the flyes smale:
> The busy bee her honye now she minges:
> Winter is worne that was the flowers bale.

Miscellany poets of the next two decades largely ignored the sonnet form, but they seized upon the alliteration here with a vengeance. The economy and vividness of this natural description did not recur in the anthologies until *The Phoenix Nest* and the pastorals of *England's Helicon*. Some of Surrey's contributions were taken up at once, others not until a generation or two later.

Wyatt's section has roughly the same arrangement as Surrey's. All the love poems are grouped first (nos. 37–113, with fifteen sonnets beginning the section). Then come epigrams on court life and the poet's own experience (114–123), followed by several satires. About thirty of the total are sonnets, although at least three were transformed by the editor from other forms.

Even more than Surrey's, Wyatt's legacy bypassed the succeeding generation. With few exceptions, Wyatt did not use meters popular in the 1560s and 1570s, and his poetic types were not those immediately borrowed from *Tottel's Miscellany*. Most of his poetry in this book comes from the two chief inspirations for his work: the early Tudor song lyric and the Italian influence of Petrarch and Serafino.[17] Both elements lacked development, or even much use, until the new lyricism of the late century.

Wyatt's Petrarchism is represented here by many characteristic pieces. Besides doing translations and adaptations, Wyatt reinterpreted the conventions in his own poems, making psychological drama that contrasts distinctly with Surrey's relative serenity.[18] By establishing a speaking voice and a consciousness, Wyatt shows how the Petrarchan conventions could have arisen from real experience. No. 58, for example, reveals the lover caught in paradoxes, but he assumes control simply by articulating them in original terms:

> Alas I tread an endlesse mase:
> That seke taccord two contraries:
> And hope thus styll, and nothing hase:
> Imprisoned in liberties,
> As one unheard, and styll that cryes:
> Alwayes thirsty, and naught doth taste,
> For dreade to fall, I stand not fast.

In no. 99, showing an even firmer control, the Petrarchan lover renounces the state of being continually acted upon:

> Farewell, Love, and all thy lawes for ever.
> Thy bayted hokes shall tangle me no more.
> . . . .
> Therefore, farewell: go trouble yonger hartes:
> And in me claime no more auctoritie.
> With ydle youth go use thy propartie:
> And thereon spend thy many brittle dartes.
> For, hytherto though I have lost my tyme:
> Me lyst no lenger rotten bowes to clime.

The Petrarchan "lawes" of love, which became laws of poetic expression later in the century, are here dismissed, both as experience and as imperatives for imagery and tone in poetry.

Of sonnets, the most distinctly Petrarchan form, Wyatt has about thirty. Many are translations; one of the most familiar (no. 50) transforms the original by its quality of living speech:

> My galley charged with forgetfulnesse,
> Through sharpe seas, in winter nightes doth passe,
> Twene rocke, and rocke: and eke my fo (alas)
> That is my lord, stereth with cruelnesse:
> And every houre, a thought in readinesse,
> As though that death were light, in such a case.

The speaker's apprehension is summed up in one terse, monosyllabic line: "The starres be hidde, that leade me to this payne." No. 46, Wyatt's own, is typical of his work in several respects:

> Eche man me telth, I change most my deuise:
> And, on my faith, me thinke it good reason
> To change purpose, like after the season.
> For in ech case to kepe still one guise
> Is mete for them, that would be taken wise.
> And I am not of such maner condicion:
> But treated after a diuers fashion:
> And therupon my diuersnesse doth rise.
> But you, this diuersnesse that blamen most,
> Change you no more, but still after one rate

> Treat you me well: and kepe you in that state.
> And while with me doth dwell this weried gost,
> My word nor I shall not be variable,
> But alwaies one, your owne both firme and stable.

Wyatt favors this structure of octave and sestet, always with a concluding couplet. Despite editorial touches, some roughness remains in these lines. And the irony is characteristic of Wyatt: he mocks the pretension of fickleness and also the further pretense of keeping "one guise" to pass for wise. The last lines are direct and rational, without clichés of feeling.

Wyatt's poetry related to the song tradition shares this directness; he prefers simplicity of phrase to the conceits adapted from Italian verse. No. 79, which had appeared with variants in *The Court of Venus,* is a quiet appeal that never becomes complaint:

> Disdaine me not without desert:
> Nor leave me not so sodenly:
> Sins well ye wot, that in my hert
> I meane ye not but honestly.

Tottel's editor removed the refrains that gave pause and completion to each stanza: "Disdaine me not," "Refuse me not."

No. 87—"My Lute Awake"—had also appeared in *The Court of Venus* and was later moralized in *The Court of Virtue.* It is sung to the lute, the traditional instrument accompanying love songs. The neatly turned stanzas suggest a repeated air behind them, but the text abandons the detachment common to song and wishes vengeance for the lady's disdain:

> May chance thee lie witherd and olde,
> In winter nightes that are so colde,
> Playning in vaine vnto the mone:
> Thy wishes then dare not be tolde.
> Care then who list, for I haue done.

The sixteenth century did not conceive of musical rhythm as rigidly metrical; an air might be freely extended with a phrase of text or be made to accommodate patterns of stress in speech. This background fitted well with Wyatt's own instincts in rhythm. His poetry from the song tradition, with its simple, lucid diction and its allusions to music itself, was inherited by later lyrics bound to music.

Wyatt's meters and Tottel's changes in them are still the subject of controversy. As yet there is no agreement about Wyatt's own metrical principles. Evidently he had a flexible pattern in mind, of roughly five stresses and usually ten syllables in a pentameter line. But the quality of living speech freely supersedes the regular pattern in many lines. Wyatt usually maintains a fair balance between the framework of meter and the coloring of the speaking voice, or so it seems in his unaltered texts. Yet sometimes there is a harsh and excessive roughness, and Tottel's editor pressed his notion of eloquence upon both the subtle irregularities and the awkward, unexplainable ones. For example, in no. 52 (They flee from me, that sometime did me seke"), Wyatt's original line, "It was no dreme: I lay brode waking," becomes "It was no dreame: for I lay broade awakyng." The editor evidently preferred formal eloquence to dramatic eloquence. To most modern ears, the unaltered line, with its clustering of stresses, is more arresting and underlines the contrast between dream and waking. In the sixteenth century, however, Wyatt was known and admired only through these regularized texts, since his lyrics were not published anywhere else.

The emendations had a different effect on the three satires in *Tottel's Miscellany*. These long poems are energetic in undermining the sham and pretensions of court life. The proverbs so dear to the poets of *The Paradise of Dainty Devices* and *A Gorgeous Gallery of Gallant Inventions* have a cutting edge in the hands of Wyatt, alluding to the courtiers: "So of the harpe the asse doth heare the sound." Originally the mockery and vigor of these poems broke freely out of the iambic pentameter frame-

work. Although some lines were metrically ragged, their ironic
tone seemed in keeping with the roughness. In the miscellany
Tottel made many changes, aiming to regularize both the pattern of stresses and the number of syllables. In a few lines both
length and stresses are altered: "with the neryst vertue of cloke
alwaye the vise" becomes "with nearest vertue ay to cloke the
vice."[19]

The variety of types in Wyatt's section should present differences in handling meter: different rhythms and different degrees of freedom and roughness in them. The satires might well
be jarring in sound as well as in theme; the sonnets can bear the
more subtle variations of a voice; the songs might be most regular of all, although their implied music requires only some grace
in phrasing, not a rigid beat. In the hands of Tottel, however,
all Wyatt's poetry was subjected to one metrical standard. As a
result, this section of the miscellany veils the technical diversity
(not always skillful) now apparent in the collected original
texts of Wyatt.

Nicholas Grimald's section is sharply different from the first
two. His forty poems include only three on love, and most of
the rest are paraphrases or adaptations from Latin. Of these,
eighteen have Neo-Latin sources, drawing upon continental
contemporaries like Theodore de Beza; hence Grimald's humanism was essentially derivative. He was a teacher of rhetoric
at Oxford, and his poetry is weighted with classical allusion.
Without his doubtful role as editor, Grimald's importance to
the volume is very small, especially since three-fourths of his
poems were dropped only two months later in the second printing. Because his work in English was not published thereafter,
he was nearly unknown to the Elizabethans. His modern biog-
rapher suggests that he was rejected for betraying Protestants
under Mary, but this view has not been generally accepted.[20] He
may simply have objected to appearing in print. In any event,
his contribution showed the most consistent humanist influence
in the miscellany.[21]

Among Grimald's original forty poems are nine in praise of particular ladies and twelve elegies. These are grouped together, the few love poems appearing first as in Wyatt's and Surrey's sections. The rest are a scattering of epigrams. The poems dropped in subsequent editions include all the poems of compliment to ladies and all the elegies on contemporaries (two that remain are on Cicero). This deletion of personal subjects suggests that Grimald may have requested the cuts himself, but others are dropped also and the remainder set at the back of the volume. Nine of the surviving ten are translations from Latin, so almost none of Grimald's original English verse reached Elizabethan readers. The weight of learning in his section contrasts with that in *A Handful of Pleasant Delights,* where classical allusion and tale are worn so lightly.

The most striking poem by Grimald, paraphrased from an anonymous Latin original, is a curious description of a garden (no. 155). Perhaps its interest lies more in what it suggests than in what it achieves. It recalls the medieval gardens of poetry, with their allegorical meanings of love and plenitude. Man in this setting is provided with food as well as with spiritual good: "Here marveilous the mixture is of solace, and of gain." A few lines foreshadow the enameling of decorative imagery in a Spenserian garden:

> Beholde, with lively heew, fayr flowrs that shyne so bright:
> With riches, like the orient gems, they paynt the molde in sight.
> Bees, humming with soft sound, (their murmur is so small)
> Of blooms and blossoms suck the topps, on dewed leaves they fall.

But there is no direct evidence of allegory in the poem. At most its implications may be like those of the natural setting for pastoral:

> The garden, it allures, it feeds, it glads the sprite:
> From heavy harts all doolfull dumps the garden chaseth quite.
> Strength it restores to lims, drawes, and fulfils the sight:
> With chere revives the senses all, and maketh labour light.

The poem seems linked with a number of traditions, but it was dropped after the first edition of the miscellany and could have had little influence.

The poems of the uncertain authors, comprising nearly half the volume, show a wide variety of types and almost no effort at arrangement (though occasionally a poem is followed by one answering it). Arber and Rollins disagree over whether the phrase "uncertain authors" shows concealment or ignorance.[22] Probably the poets were genuinely unknown to Tottel, since manuscripts frequently circulated unsigned. Ten of the authors have been identified, although no more than names are known for several of them.

These writers were much less affected by Italian poetry than Wyatt and Surrey had been. A classical background is more frequent in their section, with its paraphrases from Ovid, Horace, Seneca, and Lucretius. There are amorous poems, epigrams, praises of real people, and extended moralizing on many subjects. One solitary pastoral (no. 181), undistinguished as poetry, was the first of a kind to become popular twenty years later.

In this section especially the dating of the work is uncertain, and there is a distinctly archaic quality in subject as well as in diction. Two poems by Thomas Lord Vaux recall medieval conventions. No. 211 is an allegorical siege by Cupid, clad in heraldic arms, against the lover; "fansy," beauty, and the lady are among the figures in graphic battle for the lover's downfall. Equally detailed is no. 212, "I lothe that I did love," which Shakespeare borrowed for his gravedigger. The poem is a vivid account of aging: the wrinkles, the balding skull, and the final gasping breath form a poetic amplification of the medieval death's-head. A number of pieces preach a *de contemptu mundi* theme, several giving exhaustive lists of the world's ills. Yet most of the purely moralizing verse is practical, enjoining the golden mean, a simple life, or the distrust of wicked tongues.

Chaucer's poem, no. 238, the only undoubtedly medieval

poem in the miscellany, is in the practical vein. It seems no more archaic in form or motif than many others in the volume, even some of Wyatt's.[23] Its three rhyme royal stanzas use one or two proverbs and an allusion to an Aesop fable for this theme: "Flee from the prese [crowd] & dwell with sothfastnes / Suffise to thee thy good though it be small." Knowing the poem to be Chaucer's, we are struck by the conclusion:

> Here is no home, here is but wildernesse.
> Forth pilgrame forth beast out of thy stall,
> Looke up on high, give thankes to god of all.

No. 180, a final example of medieval vestige, is essentially a dream vision. It was reprinted forty years later in the second edition of *The Arbor of Amorous Devices* (1597) along with the work of Nicholas Breton, who was himself a fancier and author of dream poems. In the vision a wakeful sleeper sees the world's mutability. The poet's use of metaphor suggests a dreamer's imagination:

> I saw also, how that disdayn oft times to forge my wo,
> Gave me the cup of bitter swete, to pledge my mortall fo.

And the poem proves that fourteeners can be used for an agreeably meditative pace, their length accented but not burdened by alliteration:

> And sodeinly I saw a sea of wofull sorowes prest:
> Whose wicked wayes of sharp repulse bred mine unquiet rest.
> I saw this world: and how it went, eche state in his degree:
> And that from wealth ygraunted is, both lyfe, and libertee.

A more modern note is struck at many points in this section, and it is probably the diction that continues to persuade us of an old-fashioned quality in the whole. A touch of satire, recalling Wyatt's anticourtly wit, is found in two poems (nos. 242 and 243) mocking dissembling lovers. No. 260 is a blazon of a lady's beauties, first comparing her to the phoenix dressed "with golde and purple." The sonnet sequences later in the century liberally borrowed these images, and the blazon form, for imitation or play of wit: the eyes like diamonds, "or Saphires at the least," the ivory teeth. The cowslip garlands and the distraught shepherd of no. 181 also reappeared countless times, with increasing refinement.

The use of verbal figures in *Tottel's Miscellany* is another foreshadowing of later poetry. As Douglas Peterson points out, it is a mistake to describe the rhetorical patterns of the volume as new or as an original gift to future poets. The early Tudor poets did not reinvent verbal techniques wholesale, but their abundant, often obvious, use of figures, plus the large audience attracted by the miscellany, gave them considerable influence. Rubel notes that Tottel's poets as a whole use nearly every figure or trope mentioned in Puttenham's long list.[24]

Most common are devices for ordering, with less attention to figures for decoration or description. All types of repetitive pattern can be found, from alliteration to relentless anaphora. Nearly every page affords examples of the latter; most extreme is no. 251 in which twenty-six lines (having only one break) begin with "such": "Such strife for stirryng strawes, such discord dayly wrought." Tiresome though this affectation is, it serves to express the ultimate exasperation with "an ungodlye worlde." Isocolon, or repetition of syntactical patterns, is used variously in no. 284:

> When power lackes care and forceth not:
> When care is feable and may not:
> When might is slouthfull and will not:
> Wedes may grow where good herbes cannot.

The closure of the stanza with an apothegm is typical of the frequent refuge in maxims. Farther along the pace becomes more staccato, while isocolon combines with paradox, alliteration, internal rhyme, and jigging monosyllables in lines clipped by caesuras:

> Wyly is witty: brainsicke is wise:
> Trouth is folly: and might is right:
> Wordes are reason: and reason is lies:
> The bad is good: darknesse is light.

No matter how mechanical this kind of poetry sounds, it shows language being tirelessly explored for patterns. Even the two middle lines of the stanza have a syntactical variation that contrasts with the other two. Nearly every one of the seventeen stanzas in the poem has its own combination of ordering devices. The poets of the *Paradise* and the *Gorgeous Gallery,* as true descendants of *Tottel's Miscellany,* pressed these rhetorical possibilities still further.

Although these examples are drawn from moralizing verse, the love poetry of the uncertain authors frequently shows similar efforts. But another legacy of the miscellany, the use of maxims, comes almost entirely from its didactic verse. Structurally, maxims are often used as in the excerpt quoted above, a capsule admonition preceded by a description of circumstances. Deceptively, the aphoristic lines seem to express particulars after generalities, but the aphorisms themselves are the final stage of universalizing a point. Homely and familiar though they may be, they are just as abstract as the moralizing that surrounds them, though the proverb has the force of apparent detail.

Sometimes maxims are scattered in a poem more randomly than in the above example, without a logical bond between maxim and surrounding material. Occasionally, as in no. 178, an entire poem is built of maxims. No. 286 extends for thirty-six lines the single notion, "who loveth wordes, is sure of care." This truth is reiterated in terse warnings with the form if not the familiarity of proverbs. Paradoxically the force of brevity is dissipated by so long an accumulation (not to mention its irony for this subject!). The proverb was a favorite verbal and moral device of early Tudor literature. In places it is responsible for the impression of plain style in *Tottel's Miscellany;* an aphorism in itself is simple in diction and syntax. Most typically, however, the uncertain authors used mannered settings for proverbial wisdom; thus their didactic poems are a mingling of plain and stylized expression.

As a source book for eloquence, Tottel's collection fulfilled its aim in two ways. Its poetry, set forth to honor the English tongue, became a guide for later work in both style and matter. True, its most immediate imitators are in the *Paradise* and the *Gorgeous Gallery,* their rhetorically elaborate verse less vital and subtle than the best in Tottel. Considering the new lyric turn of Elizabethan poetry signaled by Spenser and even by Breton, these first miscellanies may seem to have lost their influence early.

Although poets moved beyond current fashions in *Tottel's Miscellany,* readers continued to demand the book until 1587, and the kindred *Paradise* was reprinted as late as 1606. From the number and stature of those who praised Tottel's poets— Ascham, Sidney, Harington, Drayton, Puttenham, Jonson, and others[25]—we know his miscellany remained a presence to the very end of the century. It was here that sonnets were still in print, after a long period of neglect, when the great vogue of sonneteering began in the 1580s. Those who studied technique with Puttenham at the height of Elizabethan lyricism studied illustrations from the Tottel poets. The metrical variety and control of the late century built upon the diverse experiments of early Tudor work. And the numerous types made familiar from Tottel's volume—epigrams, elegies, satires, sonnets, didactic verse, narrative, even the solitary pastoral—had continuing life throughout the period.

In its goal of refining the vernacular through poetry, Tottel's preface and collection had two counterparts. Lorenzo de' Medici's prefatory letter to the *Raccolta Aragonese* (ca. 1480),

the earliest anthology of Italian lyric poetry, made this claim
for the Tuscan language as a poetic medium:

One can imagine nothing that is noble, flowering, charming, or
adorned, nothing that is acute, distinguished, ingenious, or subtle,
nothing that is lofty, magnificent, or sonorous, nothing, finally, that
is ardent, spirited, or exalted, of which one cannot find numberless
and shining examples not only in Dante and in Petrarch, but also in
these others whose poetry you have brought to life again.[26]

Much later, but still before Tottel's collection appeared,
Joachim Du Bellay published in 1549 his vindication of the
French language, *La Deffense et Illustration de la langue Francoyse.*[27] This treatise argued that French, though potentially
as good as Greek or Latin for literary purposes, needed culti-
vating. Du Bellay's solution called upon French writers to
imitate the classics, but in the French language, adopting classical forms similar to those used later in *Tottel's Miscellany:*
epigrams, elegies, epistles and satires, eclogues, sonnets from
Petrarch.

Both the *Raccolta Aragonese* and Du Bellay's book, like
Tottel's preface, show a nationalistic spirit awakening in literature, still honoring the classics but insisting on the possibilities
of the vernacular. Du Bellay's work is an extended essay, de-
fending and illustrating, whereas Lorenzo's collection, like
Tottel's, offers the poetry itself. All three works urge refinement of language in their respective traditions.

Tottel's Miscellany proved a source book in another sense,
probably unanticipated by its publisher. It established interest
in a new form, popular until the end of the century. The subsequent miscellanies varied greatly, but Tottel's book was the
model for them all. Besides stimulating individual poets and
poetic experiment, the first Elizabethan miscellany invited imitations that developed surprising turns throughout the reign.
There were few recurring principles of structure or theme;

instead the compilers were alert to prevailing interests and framed collections accordingly. Tottel had imposed regularity on his poems, but had not extended this concern to shaping his whole volume. The later anthologies often showed a similar disregard for structure, but their flexibility allowed the influence of many conventions. Following *Tottel's Miscellany,* the development of the form was rapid and energetic.

CHAPTER IV

THE PARADISE OF DAINTY DEVICES: POETRY AND THE PROVERB TRADITION

THE PARADISE OF DAINTY DEVICES (1576) left behind the developments of Wyatt and Surrey and followed the propensities of Tottel's "uncertain authors." Poetic fashions of the 1560s and 1570s flourished in this book, and contact with an important tradition—the proverb literature of the sixteenth century and earlier—was strengthened. In the history of Elizabethan miscellanies this volume was unique for its popularity—there were ten known editions—and its single-mindedly didactic motive. Not until the aphoristic quotation books appeared at the end of the century was a poetic collection so uniformly moralizing. In the dialectic of moral and amorous verse in the period, the *Paradise* stood in sober contrast to most other miscellanies. Its few love poems had been assimilated into the prevailing somber purpose.

The *Paradise* may have been a privately compiled commonplace book coming almost directly into print. In his dedicatory letter, printer Henry Disle claims the poems were "collected togeather, through the travell of one, both of woorship and credite, for his private use: who not long since departed this lyfe." If this claim is literally true, then none of the poems in the first edition could have been written later than 1566, the year Richard Edwards died. Elsewhere the printer used Edwards's name with more flourish than accuracy: the title page declares the poems were "devised and written for the most part, by M. Edwards," although only fourteen of ninety-nine poems in the first edition were signed as his. Edwards, certainly one of the leading contributors, clearly was the primary source for the collection. As with other miscellanies, however, the identity of the persons responsible for selecting and arranging the contents remains uncertain. Additions, deletions, and changes of ascription were made in later editions by unknown editors, until the volume reached its final size of 125 poems in 1585.[1]

The contributors to the first four editions of the *Paradise* were most of the leading poets of the time. After 1585, however, the collection ceased to grow, and later reprints no longer represented current work. Even in the first printings George Gascoigne, Thomas Howell, Sidney, and Spenser never appeared, a fact suggesting a private compiler rather than a publisher choosing poets for their reputation. Thirty-three individuals are named as authors in the *Paradise,* some by initials or names about which nothing is known. This relative openness shows a contrast with *Tottel's Miscellany,* which names only three poets in a collection nearly three times the size of the *Paradise.* Twenty poems are by Edwards, fourteen by William Hunnis, twelve by Lord Vaux. Francis Kinwelmarsh has nine, Jasper Heywood, eight, and Edward de Vere, Earl of Oxford, seven. Five poems are signed with the motto, "My Luck is Loss," sometimes associated with Gascoigne but apparently not here.[2] George Whetstone contributed a single poem, Henry Disle, the printer, himself wrote one, and a translation from Saint Bernard opens the volume.[3]

These contributors are not sharply distinctive one from another. And although perhaps well known in their time, none has achieved a lasting reputation. Ironically, the most popular of the miscellanies contained only poets more transitory in fame than those in any other important collection. With their sameness in matter and manner, it is well that they have been preserved in a miscellany, where they have some collective force. Separately, their poetry might have vanished altogether. The most familiar name today (unless it be the Earl of Oxford) is Edwards himself, best known both then and now as a playwright and as master of the children of the Chapel Royal. Few of the others appear in modern editions or have received any critical study.[4]

The Paradise of Dainty Devices was frequently alluded to in its own time, both in praise and otherwise. William Webbe, the rhetorician, and his follower George Puttenham quoted from it in their handbooks and expressed praise for its authors.[5] Praise became imitation in *A Gorgeous Gallery of Gallant Inventions;* and subsequent miscellanies enjoyed the continuing vogue for the form, even though their verse evolved stylistically in very different directions.

Despite its contemporary fame, the *Paradise* now seems strangely out of touch with the poetry preceding and following it. Its development of some modes from Tottel's uncertain authors is clear, and it passed on some rhetorical patterns at least as far as the *Gallery*. Since that volume died an early death, however, the *Paradise* was left essentially without an heir. In the larger perspective, the poetry fashionable in the 1560s and 1570s had forgotten its past, and it survived rather than lived in its future. For example, the *Paradise* has a smaller variety of meters than *Tottel's Miscellany* and a notable shift in proportions. Nearly a quarter of the verse in Tottel's collection is in sonnet form, whereas the *Paradise* had only one sonnet, and that was dropped after the first edition. The embryonic blank verse (in two poems by Grimald) was ignored by the poets of the *Paradise,* as was the ottava rima. Instead, the predominant meters were fourteeners, poulter's couplets, and several ballad stanzas, especially six-line.[6]

Proportions in subjects also changed, with a narrowing of range to favor didactic and solemn themes. The Italian influence alive in Tottel's collection and later in the century is almost completely absent. The love poetry here is predominantly complaint, and often its tone is identical with that of the moral and philosophical poems. Love is treated as a ground for instruction, rather than as an occasion for imagery. Nevertheless, the

Paradise belonged to a tradition having its own vitality: the tradition of Tudor proverbial literature. With this dominant influence, the verses sometimes fell short of poetry, but they kept the popular appeal that proverbs had helped bring to prose and drama. This inheritance gives the *Paradise* its chief importance in literary history. It is a unique, and nearly final, flowering of the proverb in poetic form.

Before turning to the background and expression of the aphorisms, we must note other elements that varied the collection. Although the prevailing atmosphere is somber, it is not unrelieved. Spaced randomly throughout the book are pieces of narrative, allegory, and even mirth, giving pause to what C. S. Lewis called the "gnomic deluge."[7] This slight diversity was more visible in the first edition than later, when the added poems were predominantly of the moral kind. Even the "varied" poems rarely lack at least one maxim or aphoristic line, giving a superficial stylistic unity to the whole book. In some poems, such lines are incidental, allowing some other element to control theme and language.

One such element, whose contribution is now almost past recovery, is music. The printer's dedication suggests that most of the poems were written for singing: "the ditties . . . Wyll yeelde a farre greater delight, being as they are so aptly made to be set to any song in 5 partes, or song to instrument." None of the tunes are named in the text, as they were in *A Handful of Pleasant Delights* and occasionally in *A Gorgeous Gallery.* Only a few settings are now definitely known, the music available only in old and rare volumes.[8] Some of the poems may have had no particular music behind them, as Bruce Pattison suggests: "It was also common to press one of these popular tunes into service to sing a lyric that had no music provided for it. . . . The buyer of the book the *Paradise* was expected to cast round for a suitable tune for each poem, just as users of a modern hymn-book find a tune they already know to fit the metre of an unfamiliar hymn. Thus many lyrics became associated with popular tunes, although they were not written to them."[9]

Yet we must assume that the texts are incomplete without their music. The tedium of many long lines, filled out with reiteration, might have been beguiled by a pleasing or familiar musical line. Furthermore, a dozen or more of the poems either were first published in broadside form or were written to be sung as ballads. Verses meant for street singing rather than reading could more effectively carry their many stanzas, their repetitious phrasing, and the relentless beat of alliteration.

One poem (no. 57) in the *Paradise* specifically praises music in its power to alter human moods. Edwards himself wrote it, as he did several other poems contrasting with the usual didactic subjects. As compiler of the miscellany, he seems to remind his audience of a mitigating influence in it:

> Where gripyng grief the hart would wound & dolfull
>   domps then oppresse
> There Musick with her silver sound, is wont with spede
>   to give redresse,
> Of troubled minde for every sore, swete Musick
>   hath a salve therfore.

This poem was quoted by Shakespeare in *Romeo and Juliet,* showing its evident popularity.[10] If the tunes for *Paradise* poems were well known to Elizabethan readers, the tone of the volume might have seemed quite different for them—and probably more varied—than it does for us.

Edwards also wrote a punning May poem (no. 6) reminiscent of a medieval spring song, which was answered by someone else (no. 102) and had a sequel by Edwards (no. 125). The poems differ in mood, but all use wordplay to achieve mild subtleties. No. 6, with a note of *carpe diem,* praises "lively sappe" and "bloming thorne"; then it suggests,

> Use MAY, whyle that you may, for MAY hath but his time,
> When all the fruite is gone, it is to late the tree to clime.
> Your liking and your lust, is freshe whyles MAY doth last,
> When MAY is gone, of all the yeere the pleasaunt time is past.

The poet of no. 102 strikes a more familiar note of caution:

> Modest maying mettest is, of this you may be suer,
> A modest maying quietnes, to Mayers doth procure.

No. 125 describes a renewal in spring strongly recalling Surrey's "The soote season." Like the earlier sonnet, it concludes with lament: "I mourne in Maie, till that I may, in May obtaine my love."

Another poem relieving the volume's solemn atmosphere is no. 35, which endorses mirth because the gods too pursue their pleasures: Diana her hunting, Apollo music, and Minerva warfare. Certain formal modes provide other breaks in the generally homiletic structure of the volume. No. 76, by the Earl of Oxford, is an allegorical ballad, medieval in its dawn opening and its knightly figure of Desire, "clad in carnation colour." The narrative is very slight, but its ease and simplicity of language make it striking in this volume. Several poems are love dialogues, of a kind later so common in pastoral verse. Spenser was to make the form a light and graceful exchange in *The Shepherd's Calendar*. But the *Paradise* examples (nos. 69, 73, 74) are unnatural rather than artificial; there is no artful play of sound and sense in their labored complaints. Two poems (nos. 116 and 117) are ballads spoken by Troilus and Cressida, respectively. Their dialogue only exchanges recriminations, despoiling a form that might have had some dramatic life.

Finally, the element of narrative gives the collection additional variety, although it often falls into the service of proverbs. The allegory cited above leads to a formulated expression of the pain and joy that belong to desire. Four ballads by Richard Edwards (nos. 51–54) use classical narratives to illustrate four virtues. The tales are told with some vigor, but they are exempla, dependent upon an instructive purpose, with proverb-like lines interwoven. The most admired poem in the volume has been Edwards's narrative titled after a line from Terence: *Amantium irae amoris redintigratia est.*[11] The narrator overhears a little drama of a mother singing her baby to rest, describing plaintively the strifes in the world. Each stanza closes with the proverb in the title: "The fallyng out of faithfull frends, is the renuyng of love." The poem suffers from some of the faults common to fourteener couplets, but it also has the charm of a realized human situation. Edwards has added the irony of a child's innocence to the usual recital of worldly divisions and trouble.

Despite the elements that bring diversity, the proverb tradition still prevails in *The Paradise of Dainty Devices,* influencing both content and rhetoric. The relevant background is far-reaching, touching many vital points in early Tudor literature. Criticism is complicated today by the lack of an accepted definition of "proverb," or of its distinction from "maxim," "adage," "aphorism," and "sententia." The terms are now used nearly interchangeably, although some theorists establish categories of their own. Such an attempt is Rudolph Habenicht's:

The common proverb is a particular species of a large body of moral maxims and *sententiae* which express some counsel, ethical precept, or truth in a succinct and memorable way. It differs from the adage, or maxim, in its language and style, the proverb being usually concrete, metaphoric, and frequently rhythmical; the adage is usually abstract and prosaic. The proverb, furthermore, is figurative in concealing a "hidden" meaning, whereas the wise saying is direct in expression and unenigmatic in meaning.[12]

The modern uncertainty reflects the ambiguity of the terms used in the sixteenth century. The complex ancestry of proverb lore causes some of the difficulty; Habenicht acknowledges that his "is of course an ideal distinction, for the common proverb in the sixteenth century is frequently confused or loosely associated with the classical adage, the wise 'proverbs' of Solomon, simple figurative expressions, or the sage sayings of the Fathers."[13] By the late Middle Ages a considerable body of proverbial material had been accumulated from many sources: from Scripture and its commentaries, from classical origins, and from native folk expression. The sixteenth century added foreign sayings from its many translations of continental and classical works. The beginning of the century was marked by fascination with printed proverb collections and soon with their incorporation into literature.[14]

The history of this material up to the date of the *Paradise* may be briefly traced. The first dated book printed in England was William Caxton's *The dictes or sayengis of the philosophres* (1477), a translation from the French. Polydore Vergil printed the first Renaissance collection of classical adages, *Proverbiorum Libellus,* in 1493, and it was soon followed by Erasmus's *Adagia* (1500). The latter compilation of Latin proverbs grew to more than 4,000 items and was used by schoolmasters for two centuries; from 1500 to 1550 alone there were more than ninety editions. Beginning in 1538, Richard Taverner published translations from the work, which widely extended its familiarity and influence.[15]

Also first printed in 1539 was Sir Thomas Elyot's *The Bankette of Sapience,* which translated wise sayings from the ancients. The taste for proverbs was reaching a height when Nicholas Udall published his collection of *Apophthegmes* (1542), partly translations from Erasmus, and intended like most of the compilations for use by scholars. Popularity of a different sort came to John Heywood's *A dialogue conteinyng the nomber in effect of all the prouerbes in the englishe tongue, compacte in a matter concernyng two maner of mariages* (known as *A Dialogue of Proverbs*), first printed in 1546.[16] This debate via proverbial material was in a narrative framework, the stories of two unfortunate marriages, making it both treatise and literature.

Heywood's work was soon followed by William Baldwin's *The Treatise of Moral Philosophy containing the Sayings of the Wise* (1547), already mentioned for its classical precepts in print nearly a hundred years. Several of the proverb collections enjoyed a continuing audience to the end of the century, when the quotation books authorized by John Bodenham appeared: *Politeuphuia* and its series, with their verse relatives *Belvedere* and *England's Parnassus*. All these collections provided a context of proverbial lore, both native and classical, in which *The Paradise of Dainty Devices* appeared as a distinctive literary expression.[17]

For the most part, however, the influential works just cited were not literature. They represent instead a kind of "wisdom tradition" dear to the humanists for both moral and rhetorical instruction. From the earliest theorizing in the century, proverbs were seen as elements of both matter and manner. The persistent didactic purpose in Tudor writing drew treatises and literary works into the same stream. Proverbs, combining moral weight with stylistic example, were an inevitable bond. H. A. Mason describes a single motive linking humanism and poetry:

> Put shortly, roughly, and not allowing for brilliant exceptions, we may say that the Humanists' *impasse* was that they could find no justification for literature other than its moral instructiveness, that is, the only valuable thing they could find in literature was the boiled-down, abstracted statement, or moral of the poem, or the lifted statement taken from the poem, the wise saying or "adage." . . . And what was first an *impasse* for writers of Latin became an *impasse* for all the early sixteenth-century writers in English.[18]

The emphasis on wise sayings was severely limiting to imaginative literature in the early century. But the rhetoricians of the period continued to praise proverbs as both *topoi* and ornament.

Erasmus, in the prolegomena to his *Adages,* said he valued
the knowledge of proverbs for these purposes: to promote the
understanding of philosophy, to strengthen argument, to add
dignity and grace to writing, and to clarify cryptic passages in
classical authors.[19] The first three of these claims appeared in
rhetorical handbooks throughout the sixteenth century. Such
continuing respect for sententious expression partly explains
the popularity of the *Paradise.* Three rhetoricians exemplify
this theoretical teaching.

In his *Arte of Rhetorique,* printed in 1553 and again in 1560,
Thomas Wilson discusses proverbs under "the figure Amplification." He claims this figure most "helpeth forward an Oration, and beautifieth the same with such delightful ornaments";
and that sentences and proverbs are first among "such thinges
together which helpe best this way." He spends little time on
definition of the terms, relying instead on copious examples to
make them clear. "Sentences" he takes to be phrases "often used
in this our life, the which thorowe arte beeing increased, helpe
much to perswasion." We have proverbs "when we gather such
sentences as are commonly spoken, or els use to speake of such
things as are notable in this life."[20] Wilson's emphasis on art
and persuasion suggests the combination of didacticism and
ornament in the *Paradise.*

Henry Peacham's *The Garden of Eloquence* was first published nearly simultaneously with the *Paradise.* Its edition of
1577 was extended in 1593, including some of the material
below. Like Wilson, Peacham distinguishes two figures: "Pa-
roemia, called of us a Proverbe, is a sentence or forme of speech
much used, and commonly knowen, and also excellent for the
similitude and signification." It must be "renowned, and much
spoken of," as well as "witty, and well proportioned." His
second type, "Gnome, otherwise called Sententia," is barely different: "a saying pertaining to the maners and common prac-

tises of men, which declareth by an apt brevitie, what in this our life ought to be done or left undone." It too must be "notable, worthie of memorie, and approved by the judgement and consent of all men." Gnome or sententia here is apparently more particular than "Proverbe"; the reverse was true for Wilson.

More noteworthy are Peacham's sections, "the use of this figure" and "the caution," for each of the two figures. He praises both lavishly. On the use of the proverb: "for what figure of speech is more fit to teach, more forcible to perswade, more wise to forewarne, more sharpe to reprove, more strong to confirme, or more piercing to imprint? Briefly, they are most profitable, and most pleasant, & may well be called, The Summaries of maners, or, The Images of humane life." They are "like the most bright and glorious starres of the firmament." Sententiae are called "precious pearles and costly iewels in princely vestures." The cautions suggested for each figure are also similar: that they be not unfamiliar, too long, false, or without pith. The discussion of usage seems more concerned with moral than with poetic effectiveness. Peacham's only literary directive is that proverbs be "sparingly sprinkled . . . otherwise they loose their grace, and the oration his strength."[21]

Finally, George Puttenham's *The Arte of English Poesie* (1589) also distinguishes two different ornaments. Gnome or the director (the same as sententia or the sage sayer) is "a maner of speach to alleage textes or authorities of wittie sentence, such as smatch morall doctrine and teach wisedome and good behavior." Puttenham's examples are all couplets rather than sharply chiseled phrases. Evidently he placed moral weight before succinctness. His only guide for use is similar to Peacham's: "Heede must be taken that such rules or sentences be choisly made and not often used least excesse breed lothsomnesse." The second figure is parimia or the proverb, listed under figures of dissimulation, in which "the wordes beare contrary countenaunce to th'intent." The common proverbs, or "old said sawes," speak indirectly; thus they are discussed with allegoria, enigma, and ironia.[22]

These three handbooks show that proverbial expression was widely valued; it was held to provide both art and argument, but there was no general agreement on definitions. The only stipulation of a stylistic kind, for poets, was to avoid excess. Otherwise the moral truth of a proverb was its own justification. But several rhetorics state that proverbs should have a memorable or brief form and should be familiar. Thus the true proverb was necessarily a cliché, an expression that was satisfying because it was often repeated and acknowledged. Like the Petrarchan conventions so tirelessly used at the end of the century, proverbs were axioms for the *Paradise* poets. Originality or a striking turn of phrase was almost inconsistent with the matter itself. A few of these poets escaped the repression of the proverbs by setting them in ingenious structures or by using sententious phrases not already frozen into usage. But many did not escape. Like the multitude of lesser, and forgotten, Petrarchan poets, they were often controlled by their rigid material.

True to this rhetorical context, proverbs serve the *Paradise* both as invention and as ornament. Maxims are so pervasive that hardly a poem is untouched by them. They range from clipped, finely honed native sayings—"Beware of Had I Wist," "Promise is Debt," "Sundry Men Sundry Affects"—to brief lines with the effect if not the familiarity of proverbs. Expanded lines forgo brevity but still intend a capsule admonition. Elements of the verse form provide novelty in the use of proverbs. Meters and stanza forms offer patterns impossible in prose or in mere compilations. What ingenuity these poets show is usually mechanical, but there is a fair amount of that.

Of course, a proverb itself is often mechanical or formulaic, made incisive by a single rhetorical device. A figure of repetition or parallelism may determine its form, adding a mnemonic aid and perhaps an element of wit. The poetry based on the proverbs shares their formal patterns: constant alliteration, anaphora, ploce, and other devices are the characteristics of the proverbs writ large.

The structure of the poems is frequently governed by the proverbs. In many instances the title is a sententia, with the poem explicating or expanding it. At times a proverbial expression is set at the end of a poem, with the rhetorical extension leading to it. In no. 3 in the *Paradise,* eleven lines of repeated structure (isocolon) give detail to a maxim belatedly declared:

> And nought, but froward fortune proves,
> Who fawning faines, or simply loves.

No. 20 also opens with accumulated detail, this time exempla from nature:

> The sturdy Rocke, for all his strength,
> By raaging Seas, is rent in twayne:
> The Marble stone, is pearst at length,
> With little droppes, of drislying rayne.

The approaching moral is obvious after sixteen lines of this.

Several poems have the slight narrative frame of a father advising a son, reflecting a formal practice common in Elizabethan life. In no. 7 the son, going off to court, hears a string of warnings about flattery. Other poems (see nos. 12, 18, 19, 121) offer similar compendia of advice, but without an explicit frame. These "speeches," Polonius-like, seem structured merely by random accumulation. The precepts are sometimes so verbose that they require "more matter with less art." Remembering Polonius, one wonders about possible irony in these and the other poems. But sententiae may more easily be double-edged in narrative or in drama than in poetry of this kind. In those two genres they stand within a human situation, set off by the character of both speaker and listener. In the *Paradise* poems they are more or less abstracted, with nothing to test their mettle or expose hollowness.

Several poems of definition are also governed by proverbs or aphoristic lines. No. 21 describes friendship; no. 118 defines the world and man. The former, using repeated syntactical patterns of various kinds, enumerates new reasons in each stanza to praise friendship. The latter, which is studded with native adages, establishes the human plight by the two parts of its definition. In both, the tightness of thought characteristic of an aphorism seems lost in the expanded form. The use of proverbs gives a piecemeal effect rather than a unified structure.

Although long poems seem carelsssly controlled, the stanza in some others is a unit for more concentrated formalizing. Two poems (nos. 5 and 105) use the trick of horizontal and vertical reading to combine brevity with amplification. In no. 5 the maxim reads in one direction, its commentary in the other:

> *For death* who dooth not spare, the kinges on earth to kill
> *Shall reape* also from thee, thy pleasure, life, and will.
> *That lyfe* which yet remaynes, and in thy brest appeares,
> *Hath sowne* in thee sutch seedes, you ought to weede with teares.

(The couplets are similar to those Puttenham quotes for his figure of gnome; even lines of such length were called sententiae.) The Elizabethans were fond of poetic games, though this one is especially revealing. The *Paradise* poets loved a pithy phrase, but they could not resist expounding on it.

There were other ways of achieving the same double effect in a single poem. Once again stanza variation provides accommodation for two separate impulses. No. 40 alternates quatrains in fourteeners with tetrameter couplets. The long lines are filled out with expendable phrases, a common fault of the measure. The contrast of the two meters gives the impression of terseness in the couplets, although they too are needlessly loose:

> By Time are gotte, by Time are lost
> All things, wherein we pleasure most.

No. 104 shifts from octosyllabic lines to a final tetrameter stanza, with the same results noted above.

Proverbs or precepts are often used to give sharper definition to individual stanzas, preventing the rambling quality of many long poems. In several (see nos. 60 and 96) a single repeated maxim closes each stanza. In another (no. 110) different precepts open the stanzas, but each governs its four lines and shapes a miniature unit of moral instruction. Such a pattern also reflects the double impulse to brevity and to explication.

This discussion of structure shows some of the varied forms proverbs assume in *The Paradise of Dainty Devices*. Terseness was only incidentally characteristic of a "pithy" saying, as Puttenham's gnome illustrations show. The didactic purpose was central, the fondness for rhetorical elaboration much indulged. Besides the straightforward native adages already quoted, other kinds can be distinguished. Some proverbs are concrete and figurative, rather than abstract, and recall the distinction suggested by Habenicht: "Cut out thy coate, according to thy cloth." But such phrases had little "hidden meaning," since widespread familiarity made their implications clear. Many precepts in the *Paradise* record details of local custom or history, such as "Obey thy Prince, or Tyborne coole thy pride." Despite the aureation of much *Paradise* poetry, the volume is also rich in colloquial expression and popular lore.[23]

Biblical texts also appear frequently in sententious form, as in no. 13:

> Upon the setled Rocke, thy building surest standes,
> Away it quickly weares, that resteth on the sands.

Similes, often drawn from nature, are a common sententious device, as in no. 12:

> The aged man is like the barren ground,
> The woman like the Reede that wagges with winde.

Some sayings have classical origins, like the key phrase for Edwards's narrative poem, taken from Terence. But relatively few *sententiae* use classical situations or characters.[24]

Besides outright proverbs, aphoristic phrasing is used for all subjects in the volume. Typical is the lover's complaint in no. 16, fraught with familiar paradoxes. Many of these fall naturally into sententious form: "With hurt to heale, in frozen yse to frye," or "The more I haste, the more I come behinde." The entire poem is composed of such clipped and brief units, with no more than two lines to complete a thought; frequently single lines or half lines are self-contained. The other love poetry is also influenced by aphoristic style, although long-line measures sometimes give a protracted effect. Only rarely does the impulse to elaboration totally overpower the sententious habit. In one epitaph with 107 fourteener lines, rhetorical devices flourish bravely:

> O happy he, unhappy we, his hap doth aye encrease,
> Happy he, and haplesse we, his hap shall never cease.
> We live to dye, he dyed to live, we want, and he possest,
> We bide in bands, he bathes in blisse, the Gods above him blest.
> Being borne to live, he lived to dye, and dyed to God so plaine,
> That birth, that life, that death, doo shew, that he shall live againe:
> His youth to age, his age to death, his death to fame applied,
> His fame to time, his time to God, thus Saunders lived and dyed.
> O happy life, O happier death, O tenne times happy he,
> Whose hap it was, such hap to have, a Iudge this age to be.

There are others in this vein, but they are the exceptions. Elsewhere, except for alliteration, rhetorical patterning is rarely pressed so far. Alliteration, however, is commonly used without restraint; "searching for the letter" is an obsession of these poets.

Finally, only one poem in the *Paradise* approaches burlesque of the constant moralizing and proverbial wisdom. "In prayse of the Snayle" (no. 122) uses the snail as an illustration of several maxims. The poet concludes that he will wear the snail as his emblem, evidently mocking the pretensions of heraldry with its solemn devices and mottoes. Yet it is hard to insist on an ironic tone in this poem. Certainly one brief piece is not sufficient to undercut the prevailing soberness of the volume.

The uniqueness of *The Paradise of Dainty Devices,* then, is its place in Tudor proverbial literature. From a wider perspective it resembles nothing so much as John Lyly's *Euphues* (1579), published only two years after the first edition of the *Paradise.* Although the latter can hardly be called an anatomy of wit, unless of a most mechanical kind, the stylistic parallels between the two are striking. The *Paradise,* with a similar didactic purpose, shows most of the elements of euphuism listed in G. K. Hunter's recent summary: parison, isocolon, and paromoion (all figures of syntactical balance), quasi rhymes (jingling or rhyming the beginnings or endings of phrases), alliteration, proverbs and exempla, and rhetorical questions.[25] The *Paradise* lacks Lyly's use of "unnatural natural history," although it has many similitudes from nature. And it has much less classical allusion than does the prose work.

Some evident differences between the two arise from the differing capacities of prose and poetry. Lyly's sentences are long, sometimes sprawling, with extended figures of balance. Poetry is necessarily broken by lines into smaller units, although long measures were favored by the *Paradise* poets. Balance is on a smaller scale in the miscellany, both visually and in units of sense, since lines are typically marked off by punctuation. Versification brings a more insistent rhythm than prose, risking a jingling or jogging effect in combination with alliteration and short phrases. A prose sentence, however, can extend itself with a more varied rise and fall.

The style of *Euphues* was hardly an isolated instance; its predecessors and imitators have been noted by scholars.[26] But *The Paradise of Dainty Devices* is unique as the fullest example of proverbial substance in poetic form. Its closest imitator, *A Gorgeous Gallery of Gallant Inventions,* had no ongoing history, and by 1576 poets were already turning away from the combination of moralizing and self-conscious rhetoric which marks the *Paradise*. Euphuistic style recurred, with variations, in the prose of Thomas Nashe, Robert Greene, and Thomas Lodge, and inevitably fell to parody in the hands of Shakespeare. The poetic euphuism of the *Paradise,* however, did not directly evolve into future practice. The experimentation with principles of ordering may have somehow refined language, making possible the subtleties of late Elizabethan verse.[27] But proverbial matter and rhetorical elaboration were never again so combined in poetry.

CHAPTER V

THE PHOENIX NEST: THE MISCELLANY
AS EXTENDED ELEGY

THE PHOENIX NEST (1593) was published seventeen years after *The Paradise of Dainty Devices* and drew upon strikingly different traditions. The earlier work had been a proverb collection, set in poetry. Its substance and verbal patterns depended on aphorisms, and its purpose was gravely didactic. *The Phoenix Nest* borrowed both matter and conventions from another literary type: the elegy as personal memorial. Each volume took shape from a particular rhetorical intention, using the flexibility of the miscellany to extend and fulfill that intention. Each was a unique example of an anthology in its own form.

The Phoenix Nest, relatively small among the important miscellanies, had only seventy-eight poems and two prose pieces. It was the first and, except for *A Poetical Rhapsody,* the only collection published under the direction of a gentleman rather than a printer. The claim of gentility is prominent on the title page: "Built up with the most rare and refined works of Noble men, woorthy Knights, gallant Gentlemen, Masters of Arts, and brave Schollers." These contributors are masked with a typical reserve, for none of their names appear; only a third of the poems are signed with initials. Some identifications, however, are nearly certain. Thomas Lodge wrote sixteen of the poems, thirteen of which are found nowhere else. Nicholas Breton is credited with five and may have written three or four others. Eight were probably written by Sir Walter Raleigh, three perhaps by Sir Edward Dyer. Single poems were contributed by George Peele, the Earl of Oxford, and Matthew Roydon, and, less certainly, by Thomas Watson, Fulke Greville, and Robert Greene.[1]

A number of these poets were Oxford contemporaries (Breton, Dyer, Lodge, Peele, Raleigh, Roydon, Watson, and later Greene). Their association continued as writers of preliminary verses to one another's books, or to those of common friends.[2] As a result there is a stylistic likeness among the love lyrics of the miscellany, although it is not more pronounced than the homogeneity of *The Paradise of Dainty Devices*. No other miscellany is so nearly the work of a "coterie" of acquaintances. For one reviewer, it fairly represents "the taste and fancy of university wits" in its day.[3] And there are only three exceptions, apparently, to the familiar claim on its title page, that its poems were "Never before this time published."

The identity of the compiler has remained a mystery. The title page calls him only "R. S. of the Inner Temple, Gentleman." The most frequent identification has been Richard Stapleton, a poet, a friend of George Chapman, and perhaps an associate of Richard Jones, the publisher of miscellanies. But there have been other speculations, and a final answer would require new evidence.[4]

Some scholars have doubted the extent of R. S.'s work; certainly there is ample precedent for mistrusting the title page of a miscellany. Sir Edmund Gosse has suggested Lodge as the compiler;[5] Charles Crawford, even less plausibly, maintains that the volume is one of many compiled by Breton but nominally assigned to R. S.[6] These two contributors—Lodge and Breton—may well have influenced selections and texts, for their poems appear in extremely careful versions. Lodge's, for example, are superior to those in his *Phillis,* published the same year. Rollins believed that R. S. must have been acquainted with the poets or at least have had access to their holograph manuscripts.[7] Such a personal connection would help to explain the omission of poets who were popular at the time. Growing as they did from the tradition of manuscript commonplace books, the miscellanies frequently have the character of private collections.

The metrical variety in this book illustrates current fashions, with fifteen sonnets—the only considerable number in a miscellany since Tottel's—marking the revival of interest in that form. The most common measure is the six-line "Venus and Adonis" stanza, but a total of six poems are in fourteeners or poulter's measure. Various quatrain forms, rhyme royal, and an apparent imitation of sapphics comprise most of the rest. Like many of the miscellanies, *The Phoenix Nest* was not technically daring. It reflected, rather than initiated, prosodic developments in its time.

The title of *The Phoenix Nest* is a key to its essential nature and purpose. The phoenix legend is of ancient origin, first Egyptian, then widespread in classical accounts such as those of Hesiod, Herodotus, Pliny, and Ovid. The fourth-century *De Ave Phoenice* of Lactantius carried the symbol into the Middle Ages, where its longevity matched that of the fabulous bird itself. The Renaissance recovery of the classics reinforced and varied the use of the phoenix in poetry and emblem.[8] Although versions of the story emphasized different details, certain vital characteristics recurred. The phoenix was wonderfully beautiful, chaste, and unique, the only creature on earth having only one representative. It lived for several hundred years, then built an aromatic nest and died, usually by fire. Its progeny arose from the ashes or remains of the parent, renewing the original life.

Of the many passages known to the Renaissance, Arthur Golding's translation of Ovid's *Metamorphosis* (1565, 1567) is typical. The rebirth is described as follows:

And when that of his lyfe well full fyvehundred yeeres are past,
Uppon a Holmetree or uppon a Date tree at the last
He makes him with his talants and his hardened bill a nest:
Which when that he with Casia swete and Nardus soft hathe drest,
And strowed it with Cynnamon and Myrrha of the best,
He rucketh downe uppon the same, and in the spyces dyes.

Soone after, of the fathers corce men say there dooth aryse
Another little *Phoenix* which as many yeeres must live
As did his father. He (assone as age dooth strength him give
Too beare the burthen) from the tree the weyghty nest dooth lift,
And godlyly his cradle thence and fathers herce dooth shift.
And flying through the suttle aire he gettes to *Phebus* towne,
And there before the temple doore dooth lay his burthen downe.[9]

With its rich implications, the phoenix was a popular symbol in the sixteenth century. Its resurrection suggested Christ and divine love, while a beloved lady was often compared to the phoenix for beauty and rarity. Sometimes the unrequited lover borrowed the notion of death in flames, without hope for new life. The miscellanies contained many examples of the image, eliciting one or several of its connotations.[10] There and elsewhere the symbol sometimes represented Queen Elizabeth, "the royal phoenix."[11] The phoenix nest, however, was rarely evoked as a detail apart from the rest. This miscellany was dedicated to some special implications of that image.

Soon after Sidney's death in 1586, poets began to link his name with the phoenix. The earliest was probably John Phillip, who declared in 1587: "This *Phenix* sweet *Sidney* was the flower of curtesie."[12] Nicholas Breton opened the volume, *Brittons Bowre of Delights* (1591), with his elegy, "Amoris Lachrimae." The poem (p. 10) laments the passing of the unique Sidney, gone without the consolation of rebirth:

> Yet while I live in all this miserie,
> Let me go quarrell with this cruell fate,
> Why death should do so great an iniurie,
> Unto the stay of such a happie state:
> 　At living things to make his jewell so,
> 　To kill a Phoenix when there were no mo.

An unidentified poem farther on in the collection makes a similar allusion (pp. 25, 27):

> A Phoenix of the world, whom fame doth thus commend,
>> Vertue his life, Valor his love, and Honor was his end.
> Upon whose tombe be writ, that may with teares be red,
>> Here lies the flower of chivalrie that ever England bred.
>
> . . . .
>
> And said but what I thinke, and that a number know,
>> He was a Phoenix of a man, I feare there are no mo.

These poems were part of a larger, unprecedented expression, in verse and prose, of national grief over Sidney's death. From the universities came three memorial volumes, two from Oxford and one from Cambridge, having about a hundred poems among them. These elegies were nearly all in classical languages, and a similar volume of Latin poems was published at Louvain.[13] Such tribute volumes were not common in the period to 1602; only one other is listed in the Case bibliography.[14] But with the four volumes for Sidney, and the quantity of verse written for him in English, one would have expected to find a memorial volume in English.

The popular linking of Sidney with the phoenix, the analogy of the university collections, and finally the rhetorical conventions of Renaissance elegy point to *The Phoenix Nest* as just that: a miscellany as memorial or as extended elegy. The structure of the book verifies this interpretation, and its title implies death and rebirth commemorated by the two sections of its poetry.[15]

Like other literary terms, "elegie" was loosely used in Elizabethan England. Originally meaning imitation of a classical rhythm (elegiac), it was used for a variety of poetic types.[16] As the miscellanies show, the Renaissance elegy as threnody was often called an "epitaphe," a "dump," a "lamentacion," or a number of other names, but its conventional themes gradually became fixed and relatively predictable. Its three purposes, not always found together, were to praise the subject, lament his death, and comfort the bereaved with standardized consolations. Rhetorical methods existed for each of these, grounded in the classical treatises and their Renaissance counterparts.

Praise for the subject might follow a biographical pattern, with six conventional "places" or chronological points for describing a life history.[17] Enumerating particular virtues was a second means of praise, often by using the four cardinal virtues. The element of lament did not have the same fixed structures, but was usually used to describe the sorry state of the bereaved. Finally the consolation motifs were those catalogued by the rhetorics: "he is not dead," "death is common," "he made a good end," "he was too good for us" were typical themes for moderation of sorrow. Thomas Wilson lists some dozen of these in his chapter "of Comforting" in the *Arte of Rhetorique,* and they became common formulas for elegy.[18]

The structure of *The Phoenix Nest* suggests at once the three purposes of elegy. The first section, about half the volume, emphasizes praise and lament. The second half, headed "Excellent Ditties of divers kindes, and rare invention: written by sundry Gentlemen," offers indirect consolation for the loss of Sidney as a poet. Its seventy lyrics pay tribute in kind from Sidney's friends. The phoenix symbolism of the book suggests that the man is reborn in this liveliness of poetry, demonstrating, in practical consolation, that "he is not dead."

The Phoenix Nest opens with a prose apology for Sidney's uncle, the Earl of Leicester, who died in 1588 and had been much slandered. This piece, called "The dead man's Right," attempts to vindicate Leicester's honor and clear a shadow from Sidney's family.[19] Structurally it resembles a preface, since pagination of the book begins with the poem immediately following. But thematically its connections with the poetry are clear enough: it enumerates the virtues of one who is dead, although emphasizing defense rather than lament.

The first three poems in *The Phoenix Nest* are straightforward elegies for Sidney. They are followed by a poem praising chastity, a prose dialogue between Constancy and Inconstancy, and four poems varying the themes of sorrow and virtues. Although only the first three explicitly mention Sidney, the rest of the section extends the conventional modes for elegy. The concluding four poems in the first section provide a memorial "garland" in medieval forms: dream vision, allegory, and riddle. The second half of the book turns consciously to newer styles. The lyrics speak of love, are relatively short, and incorporate foreign influence in subjects and conceits. Imagery is sometimes played upon for subtle effects of tone; and a simplicity of rhythm and phrase often gives the songlike quality found in the late miscellanies.

The three elegies are the thematic heart of the collection. Matthew Roydon wrote the first and longest of them, combining the elements of vision, pastoral, and symbol.[20] The poem opens with a description of a wooded setting, strangely silent yet filled with living creatures. The atmosphere is serene but unreal:

> The skie, like glasse of watchet hew,
> Reflected Phoebus golden haire,
>   The garnisht tree, no pendant stird,
>   No voice was heard of any bird.

Other details symbolize human qualities: lion, unicorn, and other animals "were coucht in order on the ground," their very arrangement suggesting a formal pattern of meaning. Sidney's virtues are praised by implication in these figures and others, including the royal Eagle and the faithful Turtle. Lament is also visually embodied, in the cypress trees ("The tree that coffins doth adorne") and the "dolefull Ebonie." The final stanza in the tapestry-like setting adds:

> And that which was of woonder most,
> The Phoenix left sweete Arabie:
> And on a Caedar in this coast,
> Built up hir tombe of spicerie,
>   As I conjecture by the same,
>   Preparde to take hir dying flame.

A grieving man is then discovered in the center of the scene, overcome by tears and sighs. The medieval device of overhearing a mourner allows the poet to express compassion while recording sorrow. The man recounts the life of Astrophill in Arcadia, setting the biographical convention in pastoral and mythological terms. Chiefly, Astrophill was taught by the Muses to "sing, to write, and say." He loved the nymph Stella, and his love poetry is praised in terms suggesting ideals for the lyric offerings in *The Phoenix Nest:*

> Yet in his Poesies when we reede,
> It is apparant more thereby,
> > He that hath love and judgement too,
> > Sees more than any other doe.
>
> . . . .
> Above all others this is hee,
> Which erst approoved in his song,
> That love and honor might agree,
> And that pure love will doe no wrong.
>
> . . . .
> He wrote of love with high conceit,
> > And beautie reared above her height.

Sidney's death in war is described as a jealous stroke by Mars, who had seen Astrophill clad in armor by Pallas. In the manner of pastoral, nature immediately reacts, with darkness and the moan of tree and beast. In sorrow the phoenix fires her nest, and the mourner fears "That such a Phoenix nere should bee." As the Eagle mounts to bear the news to Jove, the poet looks up and all the vision disappears. In a final stanza he breaks off in grief, moved by compassion.

This poem bears all the essential themes of the volume. The three purposes of elegy are all realized here, subsumed under the form of vision. Praise and lament appear directly in the words of the mourner and figuratively in setting and pastoral

narrative. The biographical convention and the account of virtues are both employed, varied by the terms of the vision. Consolation is also intended, for the Swan sings several common
motifs in his dirge:

> Good things (quoth he) may scarce appeere,
> But passe away with speedie wing.
>   This mortall life as death is tride,
>   And death gives life, and so he di'de.

Further consolation derives from the dignity and formality of
the scene and from Sidney's intimate connection with the gods
and the Muses. The creatures in the poem have compassion for
the mourner, and the poet is moved to pity by the whole vision.
Both of these attitudes indirectly urge a mitigating of grief.
Finally, the elegy introduces the phoenix nest as symbolic re-
sponse to Sidney's death. And its praise of Sidney's love poetry
suggests the nature of a fitting tribute, which follows in this
book.

The second and third elegies also show the three conventional purposes, interwoven in differing ways. The second one,
by Raleigh, declares a double intention in its first line: "To
praise thy life, or waile thy woorthie death." After apologizing
for his own poor wit, the poet shifts to the biographical pattern.
Many stanzas open with a fact of Sidney's life, then expand it
into praise or a related consolatory motif. The fifth stanza is
typical:

> A king gave thee thy name, a kingly minde,
> That God thee gave, who found it now too deere
> For this base world and hath resumde it neere,
> To set in skies, and sort with powres divine.

Another stanza interprets Sidney's battle in the Netherlands
as a successful fight against living too long; once more biog-
raphy is read as consolation:

There didst thou vanquish shame and tedious age,
Griefe, sorow, sicknes, and base fortunes might:
Thy rising day, saw never wofull night,
But past with praise, from of this worldly stage.

The ending of the poem records the final disposition of Sidney's
parts, still drawing together lament, praise, and consolation:

Nations thy wit, our mindes lay up thy love,
Letters thy learning, thy losse, yeeres long to come,
In worthy harts sorow hath made thy tombe,
Thy soule and spright enrich the heavens above.

Essentially, the six "places" for biographical structure all appear,
except that Sidney had outwitted old age.

The third elegy gives no chronological account and is predominantly lament, although the other elements are present
with less force. The author is perhaps Greville, whose lifelong
friendship with Sidney might well account for his absorbing
grief.[21] The opening lines emphasize the poet's distraction:

Silence augmenteth griefe, writing encreaseth rage,
Stald are my thoughts, which lov'd, & lost, the wonder of our age,
Yet quickned now with fire, though dead with frost ere now,
Enrag'd I write, I know not what: dead, quick, I know not how.

Expressions of praise and sorrow alternate throughout the poem,
one stirred by the other. The poet himself feels grief and also
observes it in surrounding powers: he wishes for his own death,
while Knowledge, Time, and Fame all mourn a fundamental
loss. There are one or two lines of apparent consolation ("Death
slue not him, but he made death his ladder to the skies"), but
the poet remains grief-stricken. Here the primary impulse is
lament, and the feeling is not formalized by conventions as it
was in the first two elegies.

The next poem, and the rest of the first section, show variations of the elegiac mode. Besides a recurring undertone of
sorrow, they present the virtues already attributed to Sidney in

the first three poems. "The Praise of Chastitie" is ascribed to
"G. P. Master of Arts," probably George Peele. Its theme recalls
the earlier praise for one who

> erst approved in his song
> That love and honor might agree,
> And that pure love will doe no wrong.

Although medieval in presenting its figure of chastity as a
queen, the poem is curiously luxuriant with classical and
mythological allusion. It argues, essentially, that control over
thoughts is more noble than military conquest. Yet considerable
imagery is given to the "noble Romans" and "valiant Greeks,"
splendid "in robes of gold, and purple dight." Their deeds too
are praiseworthy. Almost reluctantly the poet returns to admit
that few champions are found to quell "raging thoughts." Then
he shifts to a long and equally vivid account of chastity's battle:
resisting the charms of a "lustie girle ... Whose daintie hand,
makes musicke with hir lace." The savoring of these worldly
glories as a means of praising control is nearly ironic. These are
not the austere warnings of *The Paradise of Dainty Devices*.
The man succeeding in virtue is rewarded finally with further
trappings of honor: purple and scarlet robes, laurel, nectar and
ambrosia.

The next piece is a prose dialogue between Constancy and Inconstancy. Only part of a longer entertainment presented before
the Queen, it is difficult to assess. But it does belong thematically
with the cluster of poems commending virtues,[22] and it shares
the medieval air of this section, with its debate form. The two
personifications exchange arguments in a scholastic vein, with
Inconstancy finally "changed to that estate which admitteth
no change."

The following three poems, all Breton's, show his fondness
for dream and allegory.[23] The first, "A strange description of a
rare Garden plot," contains the "strange conceits" of a waking

dream. The preamble laments a "darke distresse" in the poet's mind, which may be unrequited love but is not so specified. The metaphorical garden, a prospect from his window, is squared out in four quarters, each centered by a "knot" or intricate design of herbs. These are the knot of love, like "two harts in one"; the knot of care, crooked as a maze; the knot of friendship, like a hand in hand but with fingers apparently missing. The fourth segment of the garden contains bachelor's buttons and maidenhair, but its form is not told (the stanza may be imperfect; it is a solitary couplet in a poem of quatrains). The herbs are predominantly "unsweete"—savory and hyssop, with a pun on Time (thyme) extending the frustration in the maze of care. The water of sorrow flows in a spring at the garden's center. The poet, lying abed in grief, breaks off his account with a final lament.

The total effect is of visual patterns, of nature formalized to represent experience. The distancing of grief into an artificial world is a form of consolation, but direct statement of sorrow returns at the end. Metaphorical sense is ambiguous in the poem; the correspondences of symbol and meaning shift uneasily when pressed, as dream images do. The tone is plainly elegiac, however, and themes of care and broken friendship are distinct.

The next poem narrates three dreams and concludes with riddles. As in the preceding poem, the impulse may be love fancy, but the praise of virtues is fitting for a memorial volume. In the first dream a lady chooses one tree from a whole orchard and plucks its fruit. The dreamer warns her, "Yet take and taste, but looke you know the tree." Like Piers Plowman, the dreamer is "snibbed" as a fool and awakens puzzled. In his next dream Cupid and Diana fight for a cause not entirely clear. Diana is forced to retire, and love wins a triumph.

The third dream is the longest, with the sleeper again an observer rather than a participant. A cluster of ladies in a formal garden set one another riddles to pass the day. The first answer

is (probably) virginity; the second, courtesy; the third, fancy
with sorrow as its seed. The fourth riddle tells the common
parable of spider and bee, one drawing poison, the other honey,
from the seed of sorrow. The poem concludes with praise for
the "flowre of flowres" "whose name untolde, but vertues not
unknowne." These stanzas may have first been meant for Queen
Elizabeth, but a single interpretation need not be pressed. The
poem suits an anthology memorializing Sidney. The answer
to the second riddle is familiar language from Sidney's elegies:

> This field is favor, Grace the ground,
> Whence springs the flowre of curtesie,
> Soone growne and gone though sometime found,
> Not dead, but hid, from flatterers eie.

The third of Breton's poems is an allegory on a chess game,
disclosing the nature and moves of the pieces.[24] The sum of their
qualities makes the ideal for a public man (quick "conceit,"
reason, prudence, knowledge of enemies). The game in which
these natures interact is the world of courtly or public life. This
level is implicit in the poem, which also reads as a simple directive for strategies in chess. The game of monarchs is a lively
analogue to the sphere of temporal power, with its balances,
defenses, and tactics for advancement. The poem concludes
with a little envoy of precepts, suited both to game and to life.
The advice is not cynical or opportunistic, but practical. The
winning skill is a courtly pragmatism. The poem's final principle is a clear allusion to Elizabeth's favor, as well as a crucial
warning to chess players:

> Loose not the Queene, for ten to one,
> If she be lost, the game is gone.

The piece provides a needed theme in a volume for Sidney:
a commendation of virtues in a court figure.

The final poem in the first section, "A most rare, and excellent Dreame, learnedly set downe by a woorthy Gentleman, a

brave Scholler, and M. of Artes in both Universities," is often attributed to Robert Greene, who held both degrees.[25] With sixty rhyme royal stanzas, the poem is the longest piece in *The Phoenix Nest*. It shares the medieval quality that unifies the first section: its meter and its form as a dream and love debate. At the same time it shifts toward an Italianate eroticism and serves as a link to the love poems in the rest of the book.

The poem first speculates on the causes of dreams and laments that they are but shadows. Distraught with unrequited love, the sleeper then meets a phantom lady, described in an elaborate blazon. They discuss the reasons for his sickness, but she declines to love since she sees its ill effects. After lengthy argument he faints away and she revives him with loving protests, but the dream breaks off unconcluded. The dreamer expostulates in vain with sleep for its deceptions.

The poem has a more luxuriant imagery than the others in the first section, although its similes for the lady's parts were by then commonplaces. The natural setting offers a faintly exotic background for the rest of the dream:

> By this the night doth through the skie display
> Hir sable robe, spangled with golden stars,
> And voicelesse silence gan to chace away
> Noyses and sounds, with their molesting jars.

The debate, though long, has a clearer sense of personal voices than the earlier dialogue between Constancy and Inconstancy.

On this note the first half of *The Phoenix Nest* closes. Its three elegies use rhetorical conventions directly, then the other pieces extend praise and lament in contexts related to Sidney's life. The love themes recall his poetry, specifically commended in the opening elegy. The chess poem recalls his life at court and as a statesman. In each instance the virtues honored were Sidney's and also those of a setting in which he moved.

The poetical realization of all these themes takes varied

forms. Dream and allegory are used to establish figurative worlds with their own terms. The dreams are sometimes cryptic, though vivid in imagery, while the chess poem is more systematic in denotation. The method of the dream and chastity poems was to sketch out virtues in bits of action or visual pattern. They recall emblem books whose brief pictorial elements have a fuller meaning than their appearances. The first elegy, which carries the essential themes of the volume, is such an emblem tapestry. The virtues in these poems are not always argued or pressed, but rather are arranged as though in a garland. Around all the poems a note of sorrow plays, of loss or frustration variously hinted.

Of the three purposes of elegy, the element of consolation is not strong in the first section. It takes the form of a poetic offering in the second, the rebirth implicit in the phoenix nest symbolism. Although the three individual elegies make no separation between the rhetorical elements, the volume as a whole does. The unmistakable medieval influence marks the first section with reminiscence, while the current styles in the second show a present life for poetry.

In that part, foreign influence, imagery, and meters reveal poetic habits of the 1580s and 1590s. Lodge, whose sixteen poems open the section, is indebted to a variety of French and Italian poets.[26] Petrarch's sonnet, "Pommi ove 'l sole occide i flior et l'erba," which Surrey had translated in *Tottel's Miscellany*,[27] reappears here anonymously as "Set me where Phoebus heate, the flowers slaieth" (90:6). Other borrowings from Petrarch range from close imitations to the familiar conceits long since domesticated in English verse. His influence, direct and indirect, would be nearly impossible to measure in a volume like this one. Ariosto, Desportes, and Ronsard are translated or provide subjects; Raleigh's famous lyric, "Like hermit poor" (77:24), for example, is taken directly from Desportes. Rollins estimates that a majority of the poems in the second section are adapted from French or Italian.[28] The full extent of such influence is still unexplored, but it clearly draws this poetry into current vogues.

The imagery of these pieces includes commonplaces already familiar by the 1590s. But figures are often used for subtle effects of tone and sense. Several poems are structured on conventional blazons for a lady, with the familiar ivory brow and eyes like sunbeams. Lilies and roses abound in the briefer strokes of some other portraits. One poem (87:4), following a motif twice appearing in Surrey's section of *Tottel's Miscellany,* contrasts the spring season with a lover's sorrow; the poet is "in the Aprill of mine age" yet his "leafe doth fall amid his spring."[29] Well-worn figures govern several pieces: virginity is compared to a rose, and one sonnet likens a lover's aspirations to a ship in a storm (101:19, 60:2).[30] These conceits were still lively to contemporary ears. Ringing changes on familiar figures demonstrated a continuity in the poetic imagination, especially fitting in a volume styled a "phoenix nest." Finally, the pastoral environment is not neglected. Lodge's complaint (54:21) typically images a shepherd's sorrow in the languishing of his sheep. Like most of the late miscellanies, *The Phoenix Nest* is representative rather than innovative in the imagery of its love lyrics.

Nevertheless, imagery is often used for diversity of tone, allowing a freshness in the handling of old themes. A light, ironic note is struck by "A description of Love" (98:15), which was reprinted with pastoral touches in *England's Helicon.* The rhetorical pattern is an accumulation of metaphors, playing against one another throughout the poem:

> Yet what is Love, I praie thee saine?
> It is a Sunshine mixt with raine,
> It is a tooth ache, or like paine,
> It is a game, where none doth gaine,
>   The Lasse saith no, and would full faine,
>   And this is Love, as I heare saine.

Another piece (88:15) caps a statement of "counterlove" with these figures:

> Beautie, a silver dew that falls in May,
> Love is an Egshell, with that humor fild,
> Desire, a winged boy, comming that way,
> Delights and dallies with it in the field,
>   The firie Sun, drawes up the shell on hie,
>   Beautie decaies, Love dies, desire doth flie.

The final couplet undercuts any idyllic pretensions of this rueful sketch: "Unharmd give eare, that thing is hap'ly caught, / That cost some deere, if thou maist ha't for naught."

Elsewhere, in some of the best-known poems of the volume, imagery sets somber metaphorical contexts for love's sorrow. Two sonnets by Raleigh give the heart's isolation a physical setting. "Like to a Hermite poore in place obscure" (77:24) carries its controlling figure to such ironic details as a staff that cannot support, a couch that precludes rest:

> A gowne of graie, my bodie shall attire,
> My staffe of broken hope whereon Ile staie,
> Of late repentance linckt with long desire,
> The couch is fram'de whereon my limbes Ile lay.

Then follows a poem with similar theme, its imagery also in the service of tone (78:10): "Like truthles dreames, so are my joyes expired." Each quatrain reiterates the essential solitude:

> My lost delights, now cleane from sight of land,
> Have left me all alone in unknowne waies.
> . . . .
> As in a countrey strange without companion,
> I only waile the wrong of deaths delaies.

Lodge also has two lyrics, both reprinted in *England's Helicon,* in which setting is metaphor. The first (61:2) uses pathetic fallacy to amplify the speaker's love sorrow ("Oh woods unto your walks my bodie hies"). The surroundings are a mir-

ror, all with implications that reinforce his grief. In the second
(67:7), feeling is even more extravagantly figured:

> Like desart woods, with darksome shades obscured,
> Where dredful beasts, wher hateful horror reigneth
> Such is my wounded hart whom sorrow paineth.

All the images are clearly identified as states of the poet's mind.
Thus the second poem is plainly introspective, whereas the
first pretends to be a vision outward.

In a different use of imagery, a figure is extended by association and development into a meditative stanza. An initially
simple equation of image and object is sketched out into indi-
visible length:

> Sweete Violets (Loves paradice) that spred
>   Your gracious odours, which you couched beare,
>   Within your palie faces,
> Upon the gentle wing of some calme breathing winde,
>   That plaies amidst the plaine,
>   If by the favour of propicious stars you gaine,
> Such grace as in my Ladies bosome place to finde,
>   Be prowd to touch those places,
>   And when hir warmth your moisture forth doth wear,
> Whereby hir daintie parts are sweetly fed,
>   Your honors of the flowrie meads I pray,
>   You pretie daughters of the earth and Sun,
>   With milde and seemly breathing straight display,
>   My bitter sighes that have my hart undoon.

The second stanza follows a similar associative pattern on
"Vermilion Roses."

Finally, the meters of *The Phoenix Nest* represent current
interests and skill, including the elusive songlike quality of
late miscellany lyrics. The poem just described is marked by
a fluency and a graceful variety of line length which were
rarely achieved in the earlier poetry. The changing length of
phrase yields a controlled rise and fall, varying the almost

strictly regular iambs. The feminine rhyme of "faces/places" intensifies the natural pauses at those line ends. The same pleasing irregularity occurs in Lodge's madrigal-like stanzas (57:9):

> Strive no more
> Forspoken joyes to spring:
> Since care hath clipt thy wing:
>   But stoope those lampes before:
> That nurst thee up at first, with friendly smiles,
> And now through scornes thy trust beguiles.

Lodge also contributed verses (63:31) which may be imitating the sapphic movement Sidney had used in an *Arcadia* poem:[31]

> The fatall starre that at my birthday shined,
> Were it of Iove, or Venus in hir brightnes,
> All sad effects, sowre fruits of love divined,
>   In my loves lightnes.

Although classical meters were not a widespread fashion at this time, they had been important to Sidney's work. Hence this poem is a suitable vestige in a collection so closely linked with him.

Two poems in an unusual trochaic measure are Lodge's also; both have the singing quality in which language draws close to music. The lines move lightly and the imagery is as terse as the meter (62:25):

> Now I finde, thy lookes were fained,
> Quickly lost, and quicklie gained:
> Softe thy skin, like wooll of Wethers,
> Hart unstable, light as feathers:
> Toong untrustie, subtill sighted:
> Wanton will with change delighted,
>   Sirene pleasant, foe to reason:
>   Cupid plague thee, for this treason.

A similar movement and economy are found in the other Lodge poem (54:19):

> Muses helpe me, sorrow swarmeth,
> Eies are fraught with seas of languish,
> Hapless hope my solace harmeth:
> Mindes repast is bitter anguish.

The first of these poems later appeared with a musical score; the second was reprinted in *England's Helicon*.

A final songlike effect is achieved by Lodge in the echo poem (68:7), another type Sidney had included in the *Arcadia:*[32]

> My bonie Lasse thine eie,
>   So slie,
> Hath made me sorrowe so:
> Thy Crimsen cheekes my deare,
>   So cleere,
> Have so much wrought my woe.

These pieces have the clear, impersonal, ingenuous note of late Elizabethan lyric poetry. Their simplicity is not deceptive, although they may include ironic or comic touches. The basic influence seems to be melody, in accent and phrasing, bringing lyric back to its original meaning of connection with song. It was in the 1580s and 1590s that the greatest Elizabethan songbooks began to appear, with texts bound to music for lute or voices. These pieces from *The Phoenix Nest* reflect that interest, as its fifteen sonnets represent the renewed sonnet vogue. The second half of the miscellany, with its continental roots, its imagery and meters, shows the phoenix still alive.

At several points the poems suggest the work of Sidney himself, but there is scarcely enough evidence to assume that the editor intended studied parallels. An echo poem and one in classical meter have already been noted. The dream visions of *The Phoenix Nest,* especially the final poem of the first section, may be linked to another of Sidney's interests; in *Astrophel and Stella* he plays frequently on the motifs of night and dreams, setting the dream image of Stella beside her poetic image. In sonnet 9, Stella's face is called "Queen Virtue's Court," suggesting a new pattern of meaning in Breton's chess poem if we read that allegory as a game of love, with Virtue the queen who must not be lost, but Stella still the queen sought by Desire. The implications are many, but there can be no proof that Breton wrote his poem with Sidney's work in mind. Finally, the *Arcadia* poems sometimes share imagery and effect with the pieces in the latter half of *The Phoenix Nest*. Blazon and pastoral reflection are in both, and Sidney's meditative "O sweet woods, the delight of solitariness' recalls Lodge's poems in which setting is metaphor. But these connections are incidental; the honor to Sidney is primarily in the elegiac purpose and structure of the book.

Among the other miscellanies, *The Phoenix Nest* bears the closest resemblance to Tottel's collection, printed thirty-six years earlier. Both were published as testimony to the possibilities of poetry: Tottel's as a vindication of English eloquence, *The Phoenix Nest* as a memorial offering for a poet's early death. The first attempted to honor the language and to profit the studious; the second, to honor Sidney and to inspire poetic practice in his name.

There are other similarities. Both volumes are "courtly," the work of gentlemen and scholars. Each one claims this feature, but with reserve: Tottel by arrangement of his authors—Surrey, Wyatt, and Grimald stand first—and R. S. by his title-page claim to refinement. Like the earlier book, *The Phoenix Nest* introduces poetry not previously printed, although other miscellanies usually advertised this feature too. In sources and techniques, *The Phoenix Nest* marked a revival of dormant fashions. Some of these were perhaps influenced by the continual reprintings of *Tottel's Miscellany,* which had reached a tenth edition by 1587.

The Phoenix Nest, however, is much shorter than the earlier work and has a more conscious shape. As a memorial volume it takes form and substance from the conventions for elegy. The controlling image in the title creates a striking possibility for the arrangement of lament, praise, and consolation. No other miscellany is so clearly divided into halves, with old-fashioned and current elements set apart. The first section recalls Sidney and some medieval modes; the second commemorates him practically, in contemporary poetic styles. Lament and praise underlie the opening poems, while consolation is implied in the rest. The natural diversity of a miscellany lends itself here to a distinct rhetorical expression, the extended elegy.

CHAPTER VI

ENGLAND'S HELICON: MUSIC AND POETRY IN A PASTORAL ANTHOLOGY

ENGLAND's HELICON, published in 1600, shared some major poets with *The Phoenix Nest* and reprinted six of its poems. The intents and the backgrounds of the two books, however, were quite different. The later book represents the flowering of one conventional type, the pastoral lyric. This controlling scheme was so important that the editor freely altered poems to fit them in. New titles, speakers, or even lines were added to ensure a unified collection. Most important for the uniqueness of the miscellany, the pastoral emphasis lent itself to a rich influence from the late-century musical renaissance.

By the end of the sixteenth century both music and poetry had developed in England toward a nearly ideal reciprocity. By then, too, pastoral verse had achieved a familiarity and a variety making it an ideal subject at this meeting ground. The convention had sprung up in many forms: drama, masque, prose romance, epic, eclogue, allegorical poetry, love sonnets. But the lyric, which has been called "the chief glory of Elizabethan pastoral,"[1] was the most vital microcosm of its qualities.

The poems of *England's Helicon* came from nearly all the pastoral genres that had evolved by 1600. There are pieces from translated romances (the *Diana* of Jorge de Montemayor) and from English ones (Sidney's *Arcadia,* Robert Greene's *Menaphon,* and Thomas Lodge's *Rosalind*), from plays, including George Peele's *Arraignement of Paris* and Shakespeare's *Love's Labour's Lost,* and from other poetic sequences: Sidney's *Astrophel and Stella,* Thomas Watson's *Hecatompathia,* Michael Drayton's *Idea,* Lodge's *Phillis,* Spenser's *Shepherd's Calendar* and his *Astrophel.* Other miscellanies were also sources, including *Tottel's Miscellany, The Arbor of Amorous Devices, Brittons Bowre of Delights, The Passionate Pilgrim,* and *The Phoenix Nest.* Songbooks and manuscripts provided the remaining pieces. More than three-quarters of the 150 poems in the first edition had already appeared in print. So had seven of the nine added for the 1614 edition (these seven were from *A Poetical Rhapsody* of 1602). Whatever the editor's audacity in pressing his "ruling idea" upon texts, he had ranged widely and with taste for a representative pastoral garland.

Some thirty authors are found in *England's Helicon,* including many of the greatest poets of the age. Eighteen poems are anonymous, eighteen others are signed "Ignoto," some have initials still unidentified, and a few ascriptions are incorrect. Francis Davison's manuscript list of poems and authors in the *Helicon,* compiled before he edited *A Poetical Rhapsody,* corrects some mistakes but adds others, so it is not a reliable guide.[2] But this range of authors is certain: twenty-five pieces are from Bartholomew Yong's translation of *Diana,* fifteen poems by Sidney are included, fourteen by Lodge, eight by Nicholas Breton, and seven each by Anthony Munday (called Shepherd Tony) and Greene. Michael Drayton, Sir Edward Dyer, Peele, Fulke Greville, Marlowe, the Earl of Oxford, Raleigh, Shakespeare, Spenser, Thomas Watson, and others also appear.[3]

Nicholas Ling, now generally accepted as the editor of the book, worked under the supervision and patronage of John Bodenham, who had overseen a number of quotation books such as *Politeuphuia* (1597) and *Belvedere* (1600). There has been some controversy over the identity of compiler, editor, or patron for nearly every miscellany. In the *Helicon,* prefatory material gives the usual fragmentary information. A sonnet addressed to Bodenham and a prose epistle to two of his relatives are both signed "A. B.," and a preface to the reader is signed "L. N." (Nicholas Ling). Ling's connections with several *Helicon* poets as friend and publisher supports his identification as editor.' So does his address to the reader, in which he defends the editorial methods and arrangement of the book.

The musical background of Ling's collection was both direct and indirect. Earlier anthologies usually had had musical connections, whether ballad tunes or the part music suggested (but not specified) by the printer of *The Paradise of Dainty Devices*. The pastoral convention of the *Helicon,* with its natural inclination to song, returned this book to lyric poetry in its original sense. The closeness of the two arts in form and spirit has rarely been more marked than at the end of the sixteenth century. England's musicians were in their golden age, as songbooks by John Dowland, William Byrd, Thomas Morley, and others were published. The lyrics in these books (nearly all anonymous, although some authors have been identified) show the influence of music on their form. Similar effects appear in other poetry of the time as well.'

The bond between music and poetry was shown by Richard Barnfield's sonnet from *The Passionate Pilgrim* (1599):

> If Musicke and sweet Poetrie agree,
> As they must needs (the Sister and the brother)
> Then must the love be great twixt thee and me,
> Because thou lov'st the one, and I the other.
> Dowland to thee is deere, whose heavenly tuch
> Upon the Lute, dooth ravish humane sense:
> Spenser to me, whose deepe Conceit is such,
> As passing all conceit, needs no defence.
> Thou lov'st to heare the sweet melodious sound,
> That Phoebus Lute (the Queene of Musicke) makes:
> And I in deepe Delight am chiefly drownd,
> When as himselfe to singing he betakes.
>   One God is God of both (as Poets saine)
>   One Knight loves Both, and both in thee remaine.

The one God holds sway over *England's Helicon,* with its multiple reflections of music and poetry upon each other.

Music gives a context for the *Helicon* poems in three different ways. First, the larger pastoral works often provided fic-
tional settings in which these lyrics had been sung. Singer,
hearers, even musical instruments, were specified. Second,
music serves as subject and image in the poems themselves. As
part of the pastoral convention, music is a vehicle for some of
the poetical meanings. Finally, Elizabethan madrigals and airs
influenced the form of the poetry and completed its effects. A
number of the *Helicon* poems were taken from songbooks or
were later printed with music. And the current practices of
musical composition influenced its poems, even when no settings may have existed.

The first context may be briefly described. From the time of
Theocritus, songs had been a regular part of the pastoral
eclogue.° Although their rhetorical purpose may have advanced
the narrative, their subjects were often only slightly connected
with the surrounding dialogue. Metrically they were indepen-
dent of the whole, and in time they were detached entirely and
treated as self-contained pieces. Miscellanies before the *Helicon*
had printed such pastoral lyrics, and they had circulated in
manuscript. By the time the *Helicon* was compiled, many
verses of the type had been written separately from any context,
intended to stand alone.

In *England's Helicon* the titles of nearly all the poems reveal
this origin. The following terms for songs or dances appear,
some repeatedly: "dittie," "love-dittie," song, carol or hymn,
anthem, "report-song," roundelay, virelay, "barginet," jig
"braule," "dumpe," canzon pastoral, madrigal, "dialogue-song,"
epithalamium. Other titles imply a musical background, since
they were typically sung in pastoral narratives: sonnet, complaint, passion.

These headings for the poems contribute to the pervasive
sense of music in the miscellany. Elizabethan readers may also
have remembered the lines introducing songs in the pastoral

sources. No. 16, for example, taken from Greene's *Menaphon,*
had this context:

[Samela covered] her conceipt with a sorrowful countenance, which
Menaphon espying, to make her merrie, and rather for his own
advantage, seeing Lamedon was a sleepe, tooke her by the hand and
sate downe, and pulling foorth his pipe, began after some melodie to
carroll out this roundelay.[7]

Many *Helicon* poems imply the same kind of musical context
from fiction.

In the second category, music figures as subject and image
in the poems themselves, augmenting the poetical meanings
of pastoral. Recent interpretation of these meanings has ranged
widely. One early modern view holds that the convention was
always a vehicle: "The pastoral, whatever its form, always
needed and assumed some external circumstance to give point
to its actual content. The interest seldom arises directly from
the narrative itself."[8] E. K. Chambers, however, summarizes
three internal themes of pastoral: the exaltation of contentment, with longing for renewed simplicity of manners; love,
as the one serious preoccupation of pastoral life; and refresh-
ment from natural beauty. Yet even these elements must be
saved from cliché by wider meanings: by personal allusion,
political, religious, or social implications, the realism of actual
country ways, or idealism contrasting levels of life.[9] Hallett
Smith, while noting the versatility of pastoral, finds it basically
an affirmation of feeling: "The central meaning of pastoral is
the rejection of the aspiring mind." And its lyric "distills emotion from an ideal of content and the good life."[10]

Another range of viewpoints emphasizes that since literature
is art, pastoral is an "artificial" reflection upon the natural. A
poet of some sophistication portrays a civilization idyllically
simple. Frank Kermode regards this meaning as an opposition
between the natural and the cultivated: "the bulk of pastoral

poetry . . . assumes that natural men are purer and less vicious
than cultivated men, and that there exists between them and
Nature a special sympathy. The natural man is also wise and
gifted in a different way from the cultivated man. By reason of
his simplicity he is a useful subject for cultivated study, since
his emotions and virtues are not complicated by deterioration
and artificiality."[11] A later study reads in pastoral the tension
between nature and art which was itself a central problem of
Renaissance thought. As an imitation of nature, art might
ideally conceal art, effacing itself while complementing, and
possibly even perfecting, nature.[12]

Several critics have other perspectives. Kathleen Tillotson,
not far from Edward Taylor's dichotomy, finds pastoral "the
peculiarly combined satisfaction of freedom and formalism."[13]
William Empson's well-known study reads pastoral much
more widely, as proletarian literature with complex social implications.[14] Douglas Bush returns us to the *Helicon* in particular, and to lyricism, noting the consistent idyllic spell of
the book: "Whatever the vices of the Renaissance tradition, it
produced a body of poetry that needs no defense. If we are
rash enough to read, say, *England's Helicon* at a sitting, we
may turn to Donne for something craggy to break our minds
upon; but a continuous spell of Donne may also, if one dare
to say it, breed a taste for *England's Helicon*."[15]

With all these meanings of pastoral, music is deeply involved.
As subject in the *Helicon* it is rare, but as image—in setting
and allusion—its importance is unmistakable. Reading pastoral
as a vehicle for ideas (a less fruitful approach in lyrics than in
other pastoral forms), we find musical references defining the
"good life," reinforcing ideas of natural beauty and love. As
the lyrics are delicately recorded states of feeling, we reach
their emotions distilled through music. The balance between
art and nature is visible in the created music of shepherds set
amidst nature's spontaneous music from birds and water.

Finally, the continuous lyric spell of the volume comes partly from the varied music in the poems, partly from the formative influence of actual song settings.[16]

The poetry of *England's Helicon* is not rich in ideas; its beauty and value lie elsewhere. Social and political implications are muted or absent, in contrast with those of pastoral eclogues and satires. Rarely a vehicle for "external circumstance," it instead offers its themes directly, even naïvely, in a manner befitting the shepherds who sing them. Several poems praise country life in contrast with a king's, using music to symbolize the ease and joy of shepherds. No. 2, which soon turns into a blazon of a lady, opens with this reflection:

> Good Kings have not disdained it,
>   but Sheepheards have beene named:
> A sheepe-hooke is a Scepter fit,
>   for people well reclaimed.
> The Sheepheards life so honour'd is and praised:
> That Kings lesse happy seeme, though higher raised.

The second stanza describes the setting and mood of the pastoral life:

> The Sommer Sunne hath guilded faire,
>   with morning rayes the mountaines;
> The birds doo carroll in the ayre,
>   and naked Nimphs in Fountaines.
> The *Silvanes* in their shagged haire,
>   with *Hamadriades* trace:
> The shadie *Satires* make a Quiere,
>   which rocks with Ecchoes grace.
> All breathe delight, all solace in the season:
> Not now to sing, were enemie to reason.

The gentle energy of this life-style is expressed through singing. Even reason, not ordinarily conspicuous in pastoral, is invoked: to be silent amidst all the music would be as unreasonable as to violate nature. The theme recurs in no. 104:

> What pleasure have great Princes,
>   more daintie to their choice,
> Then Heardmen wilde, who carelesse,
>   in quiet life rejoyce?
> And Fortunes Fate not fearing,
> Sing sweet in Sommer morning.

By singing, the herdsmen declare their independence even of
Fortune, or at least their refusal to let it change their contentment.

The idea of love in pastoral is uncomplicated, though not
always happy. But ideal love, as a theme, is typically surrounded by music and dance. Gaiety and freedom of expression set it apart from the Petrarchan tradition, where a positive
state in love is at best a relief from the frustrating negative.
No. 143, a "report song" by Breton, is characteristic in its
celebration:

> Shall we goe daunce the hay? The hay?
> Never pipe could ever play
>   better Sheepheards Roundelay.

> Shall we goe sing the Song? The song?
> Never Love did ever wrong:
>   faire Maides hold hands all a-long.

No. 28, a jig in praise of love, also makes music a vehicle for
proclaiming and celebrating.

One of the most charming pieces (no. 97) in the *Helicon*
transfers the pastoral mode to a Christmas carol; actually, it
returns to one of the original sources of pastoral imagery, the
New Testament. Shepherds, lying beneath an "azure fold"
where flocks of stars are "pent," hear the angels' message of
Christmas. They marvel at the divine music in its contrast
with their own pipes. Although they sing only to "shorten
wearie night," these other voices "seeme to shine" and even to
clear the skies.

Other feelings are frequently distilled through musical allusion. Mood is established in these poems by reference to birdsongs or to the natural music of trees and water. At times music becomes a metaphor for the benevolence of nature, a favorable environment for human life. The means is an old one, as in the May song by Lodge (no. 15):

> In pride of youth, in midst of May,
> When birds with many a merry Lay,
> salute the Sunnes up-rising:
> I sate me downe fast by a Spring,
> And while these merry Chaunters sing,
> I fell upon surmizing.

The best-remembered poem in *England's Helicon,* Marlowe's "The passionate Sheepheard to his love" (no. 137), adds to its invitation the "shallow Rivers, to whose falls, / Melodious byrds sing Madrigalls."

Music surrounds poems of commendation, whether they celebrate a pastoral lady or Queen Elizabeth. Most remarkable of these is from the April eclogue of Spenser's *Shepherd's Calendar,* reprinted here as no. 6. Its blazon is of unmatched variety and richness, including processions of the Muses and the Graces, singing, and the opening invitation to the nymphs to praise Eliza in "silver song." Spenser's symbolic use of music here and elsewhere probably influenced later renderings of the idea of music in poetry. Colin's lay to Eliza, according to its introductory lines, was tuned "unto the Waters fall," "as by a spring he laye." Hence poetry and melody were both determined by the same natural inspiration. The first stanza of the song then calls on the virgins "that on *Parnasse* dwell, / Whence floweth *Helicon* the learned well." The temptation to see here a key to the symbolic unity of music and poetry in this miscellany is irresistible. The Helicon, the flowing source that harmonizes the two elements of lyric, stands as the title of a volume honoring both.

Drayton, in his poem "in praise of the fairest Beta" (no. 14), also commends the Queen. The poet maintains that the music of celebration can alter nature:

> With dainty and delightsome straines of sweetest Virelayes,
> Come lovely Sheepheards sit we down, & chaunt our *Betas* praise.
> And let us sing so rare a verse,
> Our *Betas* praises to rehearse:
> That little birds shall silent be, to heare poore Sheepheards sing:
> And Rivers backward bend their course, & flow unto the spring.[17]

A later stanza suggests a similar power in music, which now controls the elements:

Sound out your Trumpets then from Londons stately Towers,
To beate the stormie winds a-backe, and calme the raging showers.
Set to the Cornet and the Flute,
The Orpharion and the Lute:
And tune the Taber and the Pipe to the sweet Violons:
And moove the thunder in the ayre with lowdest Clarions.

Two other poetic types in the volume, the elegy and the epithalamium, formalize feeling by conventional references to music. In the brief *"Colin Cloutes* mournfull Dittie for the death of *Astrophell"* (no. 27), Spenser invokes the traditional medium for expressing emotion in pastoral:

> Sheepheards that wunt on pipes of Oaten reede,
> Oft-times to plaine your loves concealed smart;
> And with your pitteous Layes have learn'd to breede
> Compassion in a Country-Lasses hart:
> Harken ye gentle Sheepheards to my song,
> And place my dolefull plaint your plaints among.[18]

The epithalamium, by Christopher Brooke (no. 159; only in the 1614 edition), is not strictly pastoral. But its soundly pagan progress through the wedding day is marked by music, and it has a chorus of "paeans" sung to Hymen.

Nothing in the pastoral world denotes sorrow so clearly as

Philomel, the nightingale, singing with her breast against a thorn.[19] A dozen poems in *England's Helicon* mention or focus on her mournful song. Most striking is one by Sidney (no. 128) which turns a conceit upon the thorn image, adding it to the familiar contrast of spring with the lover's barrenness. Each of the two stanzas concludes with:

> Thine earth now springs, mine fadeth:
> Thy thorne without, my thorne my hart invadeth.

Music also supports the bond of friendship. In no. 153 Sidney calls the classical patrons of music to join the three friends —E. D. (Dyer), F. G. (Greville), and P. S.—in mirth:

> Ye Hymnes and singing skill
> Of God *Apolloes* giving
> Be prest our reeds to fill
> With sound of musicke living.
> *Joyne hearts and hands, so let it be.*
> *Make but one minde in bodies three.*
>
> Sweet *Orpheus* Harpe, whose sound
> The stedfast mountaines moved,
> Let here thy skill abound,
> To joyne sweet friends beloved.
> *Joyne hearts and hands,* &c.

These and other allusions draw from music the direct and unclouded feelings characteristic of pastoral.

The tension between art and nature in pastoral is not an explicit poetic subject. As an area of meaning, it comes from the contrast of poetic form with the natural world embodied there. Occasionally, however, the inner world of pastoral sets the shepherd's song (the closest it has to artifice) against nature's music. The result is sometimes the dislocation of his surroundings, as nature mirrors the distraught condition of the singer. In Munday's long complaint (no. 25) the nightingale

> That was wont to sing so well,
> Iargles [sings shrilly] now in yonder bush
> Worser then the rudest Thrush,
>   as it were not shee.

In a number of other poems birds stop singing altogether, or other natural music is cut off by human expressions of feeling. The pathetic fallacy so native to pastoral is made explicit in Sidney's sonnet (no. 135): "Rocks, woods, hills, caves, dales, meades brooks aunswer mee: / Infected mindes infect each thing they see."

Another musical artifice affecting nature is revealed in the repeated praises for a lady's singing. In no. 85, also Sidney's, classical musicians awaken nature, but the lady's voice proves more arresting:

> If *Orpheus* voyce had force to breathe such musiques love
> Through pores of sencelesse trees, at it could make them move:
> If stones good measure daunc'd, the *Thebane* walls to build
> To cadence of the tunes, which *Amphyons* Lyre did yeeld:
>   More cause a like effect at least-wise bringeth,
>   O stones, ô trees, learne hearing, *Stella* singeth.

Finally, testing meaning in *England's Helicon,* we recall Douglas Bush's implication that there is nothing here "to break our minds upon." The continuing allusions to music often seem more ornamental than substantive, but they are as vital as any other element of the pastoral convention. Indispensable to the atmosphere of the book, they underlie the lyrical spell Bush sets in contrast with Donne.

The third musical context of *England's Helicon* was the abundance of songbooks which flourished at the close of the century. They contain some of the finest Elizabethan lyrics, most of them printed anonymously but including the best-known poets of the time.[20] These collections had two song types: the madrigal was an unaccompanied, polyphonic piece for three to six voices, seldom set to more than one stanza of poetry; the air was usually a solo with several stanzas, accompanied by a lute. Performance varied, however: madrigals were sometimes played by viols without voices, or airs might be sung as duets or with instrumental parts harmonized for unaccompanied voices.[21]

The madrigal, its name and form of Italian origin, took root in England earlier than the air, although both had aroused marked interest by the time the *Helicon* was published. In 1588 Nicholas Yonge published a set of part books called *Musica Transalpina,* containing Italian madrigals adapted to English words. The poet Thomas Watson gathered a similar volume in 1590, his *First sett of Italian Madrigalls Englished.* The inspiration of these "adopted children" set England's greatest composers to working on polyphonic vocal music. Beginning with William Byrd's *Psalmes, Sonets & songs of sadnes and pietie, made into Musicke of five parts* (1588), a total of twenty madrigal books had been published by 1600, when the *Helicon* appeared, and even more came out before the form faded from popularity in the 1620s.[22] Among the masters included in the pre-1600 list were Thomas Morley, Thomas Weelkes, and John Wilbye.

The books of songs for lute accompaniment were eventually as numerous as the polyphonic sets, although the first example in England came later. John Dowland, praised with Spenser in the *Passionate Pilgrim* sonnet, published in 1597 his *First Booke of Songes or Ayres of fowre partes with Tableture for the Lute.* This volume provided the impetus for a school of lutanist-composers which had no parallel on the continent. Dowland's four books of lute songs, themselves several times reprinted, were contemporary with five by Robert Jones and with five that printed lyrics and music by Thomas Campion.[23] Along with madrigal books, this outpouring of song collections may well have replaced the poetical miscellanies in popular appeal. Their great vogue, lasting to the 1630s, helps to

explain the rather sudden end of the lyric miscellanies with
A Poetical Rhapsody in 1602.

England's Helicon was closely related, both directly and
indirectly, to all this musical creativity. Fifteen of its poems
were taken from songbooks (specifically, from Yonge's *Musica
Transalpina,* Byrd's *Psalmes, Sonets & songs* and his *Songs of
sundrie natures, some of gravitie, and others of myrth, fit for
all companies and voyces* [1589], Morley's *First Booke of
Madrigalls to Foure Voyces* [1594], Weelkes's *Madrigals to
3.4.5 and 6. voyces* [1597], and Dowland's *First Booke of Songes
or Ayres*). Twelve other poems appeared later with tunes, one
in manuscript and the others in songbooks or on broadsides.
For about half a dozen more, names of tunes are written into
surviving *Helicon* copies, showing readers' awareness or expec-
tation of music for them. Several others, taken from entertain-
ments for the Queen's progresses, were originally sung though
no music has survived.

Harder to trace but even more important are the indirect
relationships to music. Music and poetry, always kindred arts,
had a special closeness in the artistic society of Elizabethan
England. The critical problems of both forms, especially those
of measures and diction, found mutual reflection in such works
as Sidney's *Defense of Poesy,* Morley's *Plain and Easy Introduction to Practical Music* (1597), Campion's *Observations on
the Art of English Poesy* and Samuel Daniel's answer *An Apology for Rhyme* (both 1606).[24] Bruce Pattison suggests that humanist coteries, at first continental but then springing up in
England, had brought together musicians and poets in fruitful
contact. "It is remarkable how responsive poets and composers
of the Renaissance were to each other's ideas," he maintains.
"Any movement of opinion was very quickly reflected in both
arts. The explanation must be sought in the social life of the
time. The amateur who practised both arts was an important

link. The New Poetry was discussed in an atmosphere that was musical as much as literary; the madrigal was one of the early fruits of Petrarchan poetry; and the younger poets at the turn of the century were just as much in contact with lutanist song-writers as their elders had been with the contrapuntal composers."[25]

Despite the evidences of contact, scholars disagree on the extent to which music affected poetic forms. Was the poetry of *England's Helicon* musical only through its relatively few known settings? Was the music of its pastoral just an earlier version of those "unheard melodies," played "not to the sensual ear" but piping "to the spirit ditties of no tone?" In one sense the questions defy an answer, since each art evidently grew by its own inner development toward this meeting in time with the other. R. W. Ingram wonders how many late Elizabethan lyrics were written for music and how many were suitable merely by chance. Perhaps poetry had reached a stage of development making it fortuitously useful to composers.[26] John Stevens is equally skeptical, although he too preserves the question; he doubts that poets learned much from music, or that the Elizabethan lyric would have been much different if the English madrigal vogue had never been.[27]

On the other hand, Catherine Ing's study of meters convinced her that "the fact that many of the poems of the Elizabethan age had their first publication through singing is a major cause of the bold and free experimenting with metrical forms which shows itself in every song-book and miscellany of the time."[28] And a closer look at the *Helicon* lyrics will support Bruce Pattison's conclusion that "the music of every age and society falls into rhythmical and melodic habits. Association with music would create in medieval and Renaissance verse certain standard formal patterns, based on contemporary musical habits, and to these poetry would tend to conform, even

when it was not written with some particular music in mind."[29]
Musical composition, as a context, was an indirect but formative
influence on the poetry of *England's Helicon*.

Although the effects of music were various and cannot be
strictly categorized, some divisions are necessary for conveni-
ence. Hence this discussion first considers the structure of the
poetry (including line and stanza forms, phrasing, and syntax)
and, second, theme and diction. Since the question of rhythm,
obviously vital to both arts, is difficult to treat without technical
analysis of particular music, the focus here is on the poetry, with
some observations about meter included under structure.

Both madrigal and air influenced the late Elizabethan lyrics
in *England's Helicon*. For madrigal setting, verse was typically
in a single stanza, having few if any full closures before the end.
The music flowed contrapuntally with voices entering at different points, and poetry sometimes reflected this continuity in
its phrasing or enjambment. Line lengths varied, and the differing lengths were in no symmetrical order. Since the Elizabethan conception of musical rhythm was not rigidly metrical,
the verbal rhythm of individual voices could play freely with
mellifluous poetic phrasing. Even more of the poetry, however,
was strophic, intended to be sung as airs. These verses had
stanza forms more clear in outline. Because one tune served
for all the stanzas, poetic structure (as well as feeling, ideally)
had to be parallel in them all. Finally, the *Helicon* poetry,
some of which was written earlier than the late-century musical
renaissance, shows the influence of the old ballad form as well.
Ballad measure, a quatrain of alternate four- and three-stress
lines, appears here in couplets as fourteeners, or in its original
quatrains. The influence of music on this miscellany came from
all three of these song forms.[30]

Some further matters of phrasing and syntax may be summarized under structure. Madrigal music invited texts with repeated phrases and slightly varied restatements. These were

better understood through the maze of polyphony and also could be treated musically in sequential figures or imitatively by the voices. For clarity, short phrases or isolated words set out meaning, especially direct feeling, for part of the text. The echo device or key words reiterated from one line to another (and, musically, exchanged among the voices) also ensured a closer understanding of the text. Dialogue forms gave composers a golden opportunity to exchange or contrast musical motifs and moods. Dialogues occur frequently in the *Helicon,* ranging from single words exchanged to whole stanzas passed between speakers. Finally, the refrains of these lyrics owe their inspiration to music. Some were fixed repeated lines, others varied with each occurrence, perhaps picking out key words of the preceding line. Some refrains were made up of nonsense syllables, or combined these with words, although nonsense lines were sometimes inserted by composers as a vehicle for musical ornamentation.[31]

The poetry of *England's Helicon* is pervaded with these elements in many combinations. Ten poems consist of a single stanza or otherwise show the fluid madrigal form. Several of these have been broken up into parts for printing in the miscellany, but their divisions are not stanzaic (see no. 131). The large majority of the poems are in the parallel stanza form characteristic of the air. Their remarkable variety of uneven line patterns gives a diversity unknown to any other miscellany. The poets equaled the flexibility of their musical counterparts in ringing changes on the strophic basis. One example among many is Michael Drayton's "Rowlands Madrigall" (no. 74). Two more stanzas repeat the metrical configuration of the first one:

> Faire Love rest thee heere,
> Never yet was morne so cleere,
> Sweete be not unkinde,
> Let me thy favour finde,
>   Or else for love I die.
> Harke this pretty bubling spring

How it makes the Meadowes ring,
Love now stand my friend,
Heere let all sorrow end,
    And I will honour thee.
See where little *Cupid* lyes,
Looking babies in her eyes.
Cupid helpe me now,
Lend to be thy bowe,
    to wound her that wounded me.
Heere is none to see or tell,
All our flocks are feeding by,
This banke with Roses spred,
Oh it is a dainty bed,
    fit for my Love and me.

A musical idiom with strict time signatures could never accommodate these graceful shifts in line length, but the Elizabethan air could. Even though not written for particular melodies, lyrics like this one of Drayton's shared some principles of the music and reflected them. Also, lacking insistence on a steadily maintained beat, Elizabethan settings could respect true verbal rhythms, thus preserving the subtle alternations of iambs and trochees which open these lines.

Twelve poems in the collection show the ballad measure in some version, often as apparent fourteeners. Two of these are by Drayton, three are by Nicholas Breton (who had used the same measure in *Brittons Bowre* and *The Arbor of Amorous Devices*), and two were first printed in *Tottel's Miscellany* (nos. 24 and 30). The ballad-like poems are scattered through the *Helicon* volume, and some have variants characteristic of later poetry: a "hey nonnie, nonnie" refrain (no. 13) or internal echo effects (no. 33). Interspersed with late-century forms and kin to them in various techniques, these poems do not seem especially archaic.

The structural devices of reiteration, dialogue, and refrain appear so often that a musical background is unmistakable.

Sixteen poems are set in dialogue, exchanging questions and answers, short phrases, or whole stanzas. The pastoral convention had already provided scope for this usage in its song contests, love dialogues, and conversations within eclogues. The musical context surrounding the *Helicon* amplified the possibilities and brought them new variety. Twenty-one poems have refrains—internal or final, constant or varying—of a single line or with as many as four lines repeated. The first two stanzas of no. 28, a jig, show a pattern recurring in four more:

> Jolly Sheepheard, Sheepheard on a hill
> on a hill so merrily,
> on a hill so cherily,
> Feare not Sheepheard there to pipe thy fill,
> Fill every Dale, fill every Plaine:
> both sing and say; Love feeles no paine.
>
> Jolly Sheepheard, Sheepheard on a greene
> on a greene so merrily,
> on a greene so cherily,
> Be thy voyce shrill, be thy mirth seene,
> Heard to each Swaine, seene to each Trull:
> both sing and say; Loves joy is full.

Here internal and final lines are repeated, but with a new bit of substance in each. Short phrases are used as if to invite music's sequential figures, and key words give unity to both content and mood.

In a similar use of internal refrain (in no. 68), question and answer provide a rhetorical structure:

> *Diaphenia* like the Daffadown-dillie,
> White as the Sunne, faire as the Lillie.
> heigh hoe, how I doo love thee?
> I doo love thee as my Lambs
> Are beloved of their Dams,
> how blest were I if thou would'st proove me?

The other two stanzas each open with a simile for the lady;

then follow the question (varied as "faire sweete how I doo love thee?" and "deare Joy, how I doo love thee") and the answer in parallel form. In no. 120, set to a charming air in Dowland's *First Booke of Songes or Ayres,* a repeated line opens, rather than closes, each stanza: "Come away, come sweet Love." No. 29, by Lodge, has a unifying echo effect in short phrases, with key words used repeatedly:

> *Phoebe* sate,
> Sweete she sate,
>   sweete sate Phoebe when I saw her,
> White her brow
> Coy her eye,
>   brow and eye, how much you please me?
> Words I spent,
> Sighs I sent,
>   sighs and words could never draw her,
> Oh my Love,
> Thou art lost,
>   since no sight could ever ease thee.

In theme and diction the *Helicon* lyrics also show the influence of musical practices, but again the notion of reciprocity is more valid than influence in one direction or the other. Composers themselves believed in the illustrative and expressive purpose of music, bound to respect the meaning of words. According to William Byrd, a certain text was so admirable he had only to go around saying the words over and over to himself, and the melodic lines came to him "framed to the life of the words."[82] Thomas Morley made the most important theoretical statement of this rapport in *A Plain and Easy Introduction to Practical Music* (1597) by advising composers to

dispose your music according to the nature of the words which you are therein to express, as whatsoever matter it be which you have in hand, such a kind of music must you frame to it. You must therefore if you have a grave matter, apply a grave kind of music to it: if a merry subject you must make your music also merry. . . . Lastly, you must not make a close (especially a full close) till the full sense of the words be perfect. So that keeping these rules you shall have a perfect agreement, and as it were, a harmonical consent betwixt the matter and the music, and likewise you shall be perfectly understood of the auditor what you sing, which is one of the highest degrees of praise which a musician in dittying can attain unto or wish for.[33]

It can be argued that a wide range of poetry, apparently untouched by the nature of music, found its way into musical settings at this time.[34] Yet the burgeoning song tradition was undoubtedly affecting the simple emotional lyrics of *England's Helicon*. The poetic vocabulary best suited for musical setting would be dynamic and immediate, requiring little reflection. W. H. Auden suggests some examples: interjections, imperatives, verbs of physical action or physical signs of emotion, adjectives denoting elementary qualities (bright, sad, green), nouns for states of feeling, or those with strong emotional associations (sea, moon, spring).[35] Complex metaphors, ambiguous feelings, or any kind of obscurity would be inappropriate. The direct, emotionally colored diction was easiest to understand through music, and it also allowed madrigalists their word-painting, imitating meaning in musical terms.

Brevity was another element of this general simplicity. The lyrics were usually short, with images or ideas contained in one or two lines. In the madrigal, with its fluid movement toward one or a few closes, images might accumulate but no single one became complex. A song lyric typically presented an emotional situation but did not explore or analyze it in terms that could not be dealt with musically. As one critic has pointed out, conventions of the time had a positive value for the composer. The familiarity of conventional matter gave the listener a key to the poem, helped to set a mood, and allowed attention to focus on whatever was novel or especially artful.[36] The ideal poetry for music, apparently, was vivid and brief, without complicated figures or allusions. It revealed a clear emotion or contrasted several different ones, but it had no ambiguity, since music can express only one state of feeling at a time. And it had a conventional background with preestablished impressions, immediately giving even simple material a wider range.

Clearly the *Helicon* poetry fits into this musical context. Its pastoral themes presuppose direct, vivid, impersonal subjects. Its world is highly colored with natural beauty and human feeling. Any of the lyrics quoted above illustrates the qualities of poetry written for music. The poetic types most common in the miscellany are those based on a single feeling: complaints, palinodes, invitations, praises for a lady (including blazons), or dance songs of pure merriment. There are of course exceptions to these basically musical characteristics. Bartholomew Yong's translations are often long and heavy with words. Other long poems are composed entirely of brief, pictorial elements, like Spenser's praise of Queen Elizabeth (no. 6). Sidney's lyrics are frequently more subtle than others in the book. In no. 3, for example, "Ring out your belles, let mourning shewes be spread," he gives the refrain an ironic turn, shifting to mockery of an uncertain direction:

> From so ungratefull fancie,
> From such a femall frenzie,
> From them that use men thus:
> Good Lord deliver us,

becomes in the last stanza:

> Therefore from so vile fancie,
> To call such wit a frenzie,
> Who love can temper thus:
> Good Lord deliver us.

But the practices of musical composition left their mark on much of the *Helicon* poetry. The reciprocity of the two arts was lively in 1600 and the pastoral emphasis invited the meeting in this book. Among the miscellanies, *England's Helicon* has perhaps the narrowest focus, bounded by a single convention. But the musical background provides both implications of meaning and diversity of form. In addition, it reminds us that Elizabethan readers experienced a dimension in these lyrics now unfamiliar unless we hear the settings. Even then, the pervasive atmosphere of song behind the verses is difficult for us to reconstruct. In this book, if anywhere, the sixteenth century recaptured the original multiple sense of lyric poetry.

CHAPTER VII

THE MISCELLANIES AND THE AGE

THE ELIZABETHAN MISCELLANIES, as a phenomenon, defy a simple description. Few generalizations about form and substance can embrace them all. Yet they were abundant, popular, and often influential on one another and on wider poetic practice. From the total of about twenty multiple-author collections, one was being printed or reprinted in nearly every year of Elizabeth's reign. Their audiences varied so widely that almost any reader of the time would have been familiar with at least one miscellany, or with parts of one.

In length, purpose, composition, structure, and audience, the miscellanies show their diversity. They range in size from Tottel's 310 poems to the half dozen in *A Small Handful of Fragrant Flowers.* Nearly all include prefatory statements by editors or printers, claiming various intentions or principles of selection. Often the anthologies are said to be both pithy and pleasant, combining gravity with delight. For a book like *The Paradise of Dainty Devices,* this meant the pleasure of moral soundness, while Richard Jones permits a wider diversity in *Brittons Bowre of Delights,* with poems "some of worthines, and some of wantonnes." Several prefaces include defenses of poetry or of the English tongue, implying that their books stand as vindications. Timothe Kendall, in *Flowers of Epigrams,* first argues for the profit and pleasure of poetry, but insists on the seriousness of his own choices: "I have left the lewde, I have chosen the chaste: I have weeded away all wanton and woorthlesse woordes: I have pared away all pernicious patches: I have chipt & chopt of all beastly boughes and branches, all filthy and fulsom phrases."[1] In contrast, the preface to *A Poetical Rhapsody* defends its love poetry as a whetstone to wit and a spur to generous actions. These opening statements seem revealing of purpose, but they are often public relations or advertising pieces, sometimes presenting a "facade of morality" to potential buyers.[2]

The miscellanies also vary widely in composition. The four discussed here show differing principles: *Tottel's Miscellany* aimed for diversity of poetic types; *The Paradise of Dainty Devices* drew upon the proverb tradition for its more homogeneous substance and related styles; *The Phoenix Nest* used the rhetoric of elegy, and also contrasted archaic elements with the newer fashions in lyric associated with Sidney; *England's Helicon,* bounded by the pastoral convention, took from the late-century songbooks both its texts and the wider influences of musical composition upon poetry.

Other areas of Elizabethan interest helped to determine the composition of some collections. Balladry was the foundation of *A Handful of Pleasant Delights,* and it contributed both popular and courtly songs to many other miscellanies. Old concepts of tragedy permeate *A Mirror for Magistrates,* an anomalous relative of the multiple-author volumes. And classical forms or translations, along with imitations of continental poetry, gave important substance to *Tottel's Miscellany, A Poetical Rhapsody,* and others. The late-century dictionaries of quotations and sententiae led to such poetic counterparts as *Belvedere* and *England's Parnassus.* Music had a connection with nearly every miscellany, and fiction and plays contributed incidental poems.

In structure as in these other aspects, the miscellanies never developed a repeated convention. Few have an apparently careful order, although *The Phoenix Nest* is an exception. *Tottel's Miscellany* is divided into sections according to its poets, and within the sections the poems are sometimes grouped by types. *A Poetical Rhapsody,* last of the collections, returns to Tottel's plan of division according to poets.

The chronology of the poems never seems to determine order,

and in most collections the majority of poems are unsigned, so editors did not arrange them by identification. The origins of some miscellanies may explain their random structure, for many came from private gatherings in commonplace books, which were largely a result of poets' reluctance to appear in print. Publishers may have acquired manuscript collections accumulated over varying lengths of time and then printed them without reordering. It is less likely that the later miscellanies grew this way, since poets became more willing to claim their work, and the pieces in late collections were often taken from printed sources.

The closest parallel to the miscellany among Elizabethan literary forms is the sonnet sequence, another composite work of flexible length. But the differences between them are greater than the similarities. The sixteenth-century sequences all had love as a subject, with an essentially Petrarchan background either assimilated or reacted against. The miscellanies, with their much wider range of subject, never evolved toward the conventions possible when thematic material is repeated. Characteristic rhetorical patterns in the sonnet sequences reached a fine subtlety in the hands of Spenser, Sidney, and Shakespeare. These sequences, and the others to some extent, have a narrative, discursive progression, with development of tone and persona possible because they are single-author works and because the sonnet is a consistent form throughout. The miscellanies, with varied poetic forms and authors in each volume, had no internal basis for structure. Instead, they had to borrow external principles for unity—the proverb tradition, pastoral, or balladry—which gave little guidance in ordering the collections.[8]

Finally, the audiences for miscellanies varied greatly. *Tottel's Miscellany* was obviously read by poets, whereas the *Paradise,* most reprinted of all the anthologies, did not influence poetic practice after its time. Yet it was widely popular and the diversity of its readers can only be guessed. Buyers of broadsides made up much of the audience for *A Handful of Pleasant Delights,* but its verse had courtly connections as well as popular. More distinctly courtly were the two anthologies Richard Jones ascribed to Breton—*Brittons Bowre of Delights* and *The Arbor of Amorous Devices*—whose prefaces addressed "gentlemen readers" and whose acrostic compliments to court ladies indicated an aristocratic audience. Whatever their particular targets, publishers recognized the miscellany as a potentially salable form and wooed readers in many ways. They imitated one another's collections, puffed their title pages with claims, ascribed a whole book to a single popular poet, or possibly, as in one instance, falsely implied multiple authorship simply for the added appeal. As part of a lively book trade, some miscellany or other touched the reading habits of nearly every potential buyer.

Seen as a whole, the history of all the miscellanies makes its own revelations. The miscellany was almost exclusively an Elizabethan form, running from 1557 to 1602 (except for *The Court of Venus* fragments from perhaps the 1530s and the reprints extending into the seventeenth century). Its possible origin as a form in manuscript collections coming into print has been noted. The end of the lyric anthologies in 1602, followed only by very dissimilar books of satire, translations, or political verse, is harder to account for. Perhaps readers turned to the songbooks popular from the 1590s into the 1630s, a direction *England's Helicon* pointed in 1600. Lyric poetry continued to be published abundantly in songbooks, with a nearly inseparable musical counterpart.

The span of the miscellanies reveals many shifts and developments in poetic practice but no simple progression. They usually were conservative rather than innovative, and many included meters, subjects, and rhetorical devices past their freshness or vogue. Since dating is often hard to establish for the poems, no chronological progress can be charted from one volume to the next. Moreover, many collections included pieces written long before the time of compilation. *A Poetical Rhapsody* prints verse from a span of twenty-five years; *Tottel's Miscellany* includes a poem by Chaucer, and it may have others unexpectedly early as well.

Establishing patterns of taste from the miscellanies is equally difficult. They ranged from didactic to light, courtly to popular, with many of them showing a mixture of these appeals. At any point in the century several very different ones were in demand and were available in recent editions. If anything, they reveal the gap between styles being written and experimented with, on the one hand, and older fashions still favored by the reading public on the other.

Still, a few generalizations about the progress of the miscellanies can be made. The first ones introduced pieces not yet published, while the last ones had a higher proportion of work already printed elsewhere. Yet publishers continued to claim that their poems were "never before imprinted." Apparently, as more writers were willingly (or with only feigned reluctance) consenting to publication, compilers had more printed sources to draw upon, but they wanted also to retain the appeal of the unfamiliar.

The dialectic of moral and amorous verse begun by reactions to *The Court of Venus* continued, with some defenses or expressions of righteous indignation included in later prefaces. *Tottel's Miscellany* shared both the homiletic vein and love poetry, itself often somber in tone. The two types of verse developed in different ways, easily traced in the miscellanies. The sonnet form was renewed in love poetry after infrequent use in the three or four decades following Wyatt and Surrey. The pastoral convention gained in prominence, while its gaiety and naïveté in lyric contrasted with the rhetorically more subtle verse of *The Phoenix Nest* and *A Poetical Rhapsody*.

In the meantime the didactic strain shifted from euphuistic

poems to a distillation of aphoristic expression at the end of the century. The quotation books overseen by John Bodenham, sometimes transforming verse lines into prose and vice versa, rejected the ornamentation favored by *Paradise* and *Gorgeous Gallery* poets. In these late collections poetry borders on prose, as in *England's Helicon* it touches the nature of music.

The Elizabethan miscellanies, then, though not widely read today, deserve rediscovery and reassessment. They cannot fairly be called a genre, and they developed few aesthetic principles as a form. But they present many interests to the student of Elizabethan poetry. Historically, they provide an index of trends in theme and technique, although an index to be read cautiously and interpreted broadly. The quantity and the dates of reprints offer sometimes surprising evidence in the history of taste. Details of compilation, editing, and publication shed light on practices of a flourishing, competitive book trade.

The miscellanies repay critical attention as well as historical study. Much of their poetry is still admired and is often reprinted, having weathered shifts of sensibility to reach our own impermanent preferences. Some volumes preserve poetry that would otherwise have been lost or is still undiscovered anywhere else. Individual collections gave a new incarnation to literary conventions of the period. A significant presence in their own time, the miscellanies are still suggestive and attractive reading.

NOTES

ABBREVIATIONS

DNB	*Dictionary of National Biography*
ELH	*English Literary History*
HLB	*Huntington Library Bulletin*
HLQ	*Huntington Library Quarterly*
JAMS	*Journal of the American Musicological Society*
JEGP	*Journal of English and Germanic Philology*
MLN	*Modern Language Notes*
MLQ	*Modern Language Quarterly*
MLR	*Modern Language Review*
MP	*Modern Philology*
N&Q	*Notes and Queries*
OED	*Oxford English Dictionary*
PMLA	*Publications of the Modern Language Association*
PQ	*Philological Quarterly*
RES	*Review of English Studies*
SAQ	*South Atlantic Quarterly*
SB	*Studies in Bibliography*
SP	*Studies in Philology*
STC	*Short Title Catalogue*
TLS	*Times Literary Supplement*

NOTES TO CHAPTER I

The Development of the Miscellanies to 1590

[1] Hyder E. Rollins, ed., *Tottel's Miscellany*, 2d ed., rev. (Cambridge, Mass., 1965), II, 108.

[2] There are two bibliographies of these collections: Arthur E. Case, *A Bibliography of English Poetical Miscellanies, 1521–1750* (Oxford, 1935); Hyder E. Rollins, "Miscellanies and Representative Ballad Collections, 1557–1660," in *The Cambridge Bibliography of English Literature* (Cambridge, 1940), Vol. I. Case includes foreign-language collections and omits those ascribed to a single author, even though they were clearly known as composite works when published. Rollins does not limit his list to multiple authorship. Both bibliographies are useful but incomplete, as are the accounts in J. William Hebel and Hoyt H. Hudson, "Notes to Elizabethan Miscellanies," in *Poetry of the English Renaissance, 1509–1660* (New York, 1952), pp. 947–950, and in C. S. Lewis's bibliography of sixteenth-century verse collections, in *English Literature in the Sixteenth Century, Excluding Drama* (Oxford, 1954), pp. 600–601. The *OED* records the first use of the term "miscellany" with the present meaning in 1638.

[3] For a description of some anthologies, see Franklin Dickey, "Collections of Songs and Sonnets," in *Elizabethan Poetry*, ed. John Russell Brown and Bernard Harris (London, 1960), pp. 50–51; John Erskine, *The Elizabethan Lyric* (New York, 1931), pp. 56–71; Henry Huth, *Inedited Poetical Miscellanies, 1584–1700* (London, 1870). Important manuscripts containing Wyatt poems are described in Raymond Southall, *The Courtly Maker: An Essay on the Poetry of Wyatt and His Contemporaries* (New York, 1964), pp. 15–25, 160–173, and in his "The Devonshire Manuscript Collection of Early Tudor Poetry, 1532–41," *RES*, n.s., XV (1964), 142–150. The Harrington manuscript of Arundel Castle, gathered over two generations (ca. 1555–1600), is especially valuable; it is printed in Ruth Hughey, ed., *The Arundel Harington Manuscript of Tudor Poetry*, 2 vols. (Columbus, O., 1960).

[4] George Wither, *The Schollers Purgatory* (*STC* 25919), pp. 121–122. General background on the relationship of writer, publisher, and audience in the age is found in H. S. Bennett, *English Books and Readers, 1558–1603* (Cambridge, 1965); Edwin H. Miller, *The Professional Writer in Elizabethan England* (Cambridge, Mass., 1959); and Phoebe Sheavyn, *The Literary Profession in the Elizabethan Age*, 2d ed., rev. (New York, 1967).

[5] In about 1480 Lorenzo de' Medici sent to Ferdinand of Aragon, son of the king of Naples, at Ferdinand's request a collection of Tuscan poems now known as the *Raccolta Aragonese*. This volume, with 450 poems by thirty different poets, was the first general anthology of Italian lyric poetry and included a prefatory letter (and some poems) by Lorenzo himself.

Several other collections of early Italian lyric verse were published shortly before and after 1530. In 1545 appeared the first similar anthology of recent poetry, *Rime diverse di molti eccellentiss. Auttori nuovamente raccolte, libro primo*. It was reprinted in each of the two following years, and a *Libro secondo* was published in 1547. Other publishers followed suit, and more than a score of anthologies, in original or reprinted editions, had appeared by 1570. For a list of complete titles in the original series, see the *British Museum General Catalogue of Printed Books*, 54 (London, 1960), 399. For further details, see Ernest Hatch Wilkins, *A History of Italian Literature* (Cambridge, Mass., 1954), pp. 146–147, 294–251. Wilkins believes "it was almost wholly through these editions and these anthologies that the poetry of Petrarch and the

Petrarchistic Italian lyric of the sixteenth century came to the knowledge of foreign visitors," who took copies home with them (p. 250).

⁶ For the publication history, see Russell A. Fraser, ed., *The Court of Venus* (Durham, N.C., 1955), pp. 1–46. Fraser summarizes earlier theories about the fragments, including *TLS* correspondence and R. H. Griffith and R. A. Law, " 'A Boke of Balettes' and 'The Courte of Venus,' " *University of Texas Studies in English*, no. 10 (1930), pp. 5–12, written after the discovery in 1929 of the Stark fragment, bound in the endpapers of a sixteenth-century translation of More's *Utopia*.

⁷ See Russell A. Fraser, "Political Prophecy in *The Pilgrim's Tale*," *SAQ*, LVI (1957), 67–78.

⁸ Fraser's introduction to *The Court of Venus*, p. 34; but see Charles A. Huttar, "Wyatt and the Several Editions of the *Court of Venus*," *SB*, XIX (1966), 181–195.

⁹ A. K. Foxwell, ed., *The Poems of Sir Thomas Wiat* (London, 1913), II, 172.

¹⁰ John Hall, quoted in Fraser, ed., *Court of Venus*, p. 57.

¹¹ *The Court of Virtue*, ed. Russell A. Fraser (New Brunswick, N.J., 1961).

¹² Dickey, "Collections of Songs and Sonnets," p. 32; Lily Bess Campbell, *Divine Poetry and Drama in Sixteenth Century England* (Cambridge, 1959), p. 47.

¹³ Fraser, ed., *The Court of Venus*, pp. 56–73, traces some of these connections and cites known references to the book.

¹⁴ See, for details, Hallett Smith, "English Metrical Psalms in the Sixteenth Century and their Literary Significance," *HLQ*, IX, 3 (May 1946), 249–271, and Campbell, *Divine Poetry and Drama*, pp. 34–73. A miscellany consisting basically of scriptural translations is discussed in Charles A. Huttar, "Poems by Surrey and Others in a Printed Miscellany circa 1550," *English Miscellany*, XVI (1965), 9–18.

¹⁵ For this and subsequent miscellanies, all editions up to 1603 are noted; the most recent edition is cited in full. There were two editions of *Tottel's Miscellany* in 1557, two in 1559, and one each in 1565, 1567, 1574, 1585, and 1587. See the description of these and all later editions in Rollins, ed., *Tottel's Miscellany*, II, 7–65.

¹⁶ See *ibid.*, pp. 92–101.

¹⁷ See H. E. Rollins, "Tottel's 'Miscellany' and John Hall," *TLS*, 14 Jan. 1932, p. 28.

¹⁸ An earlier version of the *Mirror for Magistrates*, bound with John Lydgate's *Falls of Princes*, had in 1554 or 1555 included the lives of some contemporaries. This printing was prohibited by Queen Mary's chancellor, and the book was first published separately in 1559. For an account of editions to 1587, the last one to follow the original arrangement, see Lily B. Campbell, ed., *The Mirror for Magistrates* (Cambridge, 1938), pp. 4–20. See also Lily B. Campbell, ed., *Parts Added to the Mirror for Magistrates* (Cambridge, 1946).

¹⁹ See introduction to Hyder E. Rollins, ed., *A Handful of Pleasant Delights* (New York, 1965). See also Hyder E. Rollins, "The Date, Authors, and Contents of *A Handful of Pleasant Delights*," *JEGP*, XVIII (1919), 43–59. Rollins describes a fragment of the miscellany found bound into the endpapers of a contemporary volume when it was acquired by the Huntington Library ("*A Handful of Pleasant Delights*," *MLN*, XLI, 5 [May 1926], 327).

²⁰ For general background on the ballads, see David C. Fowler, *A Literary History of the Popular Ballad* (Durham, N.C., 1968); Albert B. Friedman, *The Ballad Revival: Studies in the Influence of Popular on Sophisticated Poetry* (Chicago, 1961); Hyder E. Rollins, "The Black-Letter Broadside Ballad," *PMLA*, XXXIV (1919), 258–339; and Leslie Shepard, *The Broadside Ballad: A Study in Origins and Meaning* (London, 1962). In "Music for *A Handefull of pleasant delites*," *JAMS*, X (1937), 151–180, John Ward describes the sources and background of the tunes in this collection, printing some examples. In the chapter "Ballad and Dance" in *Music and Poetry of the English Renaissance* (London, 1948), pp. 160–190, Bruce Pattison also identifies tunes for poems in several miscellanies and prints a number of them.

²¹ Rollins, ed., *Tottel's Miscellany*, II, 109–110. See also Hyder E. Rollins, *An*

Analytical Index to the Ballad-Entries (1557–1709) in the Registers of the Company of Stationers of London (University of North Carolina, 1924).

[22] Quoted in Sheavyn, *Literary Profession*, p. 153; and in Ben Jonson, *Works*, ed. C. H. Herford and Percy Simpson, I (Oxford, 1925), 145. See Guy Andrew Thompson, *Elizabethan Criticism of Poetry* (Menasha, Wis., 1914), pp. 9–19, for attacks on ballad writers.

[23] Rollins, ed., *A Handful of Pleasant Delights*, p. ix.

[24] C. R. Baskervill, "Three Books Edited by H. E. Rollins, Reviewed," *MP*, XXIII (Aug. 1925), 119–125. The three works reviewed are *Cavalier and Puritan Ballads and Broadsides Illustrating the Period of the Great Rebellion, 1640–1660*, the edition of *A Handful of Pleasant Delights*, and *An Analytical Index to the Ballad-Entries*. Pattison ("Ballad and Dance," pp. 162–164) also discusses the lack of rigid separation between popular and cultured ballads in origin, content, and tunes.

[25] The only reprinting of *A Small Handful of Fragrant Flowers* was edited by Thomas Park in *Heliconia*, I, 2 (London, 1815). Hyder E. Rollins ("*A Small Handful of Fragrant Flowers*," *HLB*, IX [1936], 27–35) argues against Breton's authorship of the book, as does Breton's nineteenth-century editor, Alexander B. Grosart (*The Works in Verse and Prose of Nicholas Breton*, 2 vols. [Edinburgh, 1879], I, lxxiii). For a counterargument see Jean Robertson, ed., *Poems by Nicholas Breton (Not Hitherto Reprinted)* (Liverpool, 1952), pp. xxxiii–xxxvii.

[26] Editions appeared in 1577, 1578, 1580, 1585, 1590, 1596(2), 1600, 1606. For a description of them see Hyder E. Rollins, ed., *The Paradise of Dainty Devices* (Cambridge, Mass., 1927), pp. xiv–xxxi.

[27] The only reprint of *Flowers of Epigrams* was published by the Spenser Society in 1874. For a discussion of Kendall's borrowings see H. B. Lathrop, "James Cornarius's *Selecta Epigrammata Graeca* and the Early English Epigrammatists," *MLN*, XLIII, 4 (April 1928), 223–229.

[28] There is no evidence that the *Greek Anthology* was translated into English in the sixteenth century, although one of Kendall's sections is entitled "Flowers Out of Certaine Greek Aucthours." See John Edwin Sandys, *A History of Classical Scholarship* (Cambridge, 1908), II, 228–233.

[29] Hyder E. Rollins, ed., *A Gorgeous Gallery of Gallant Inventions* (Cambridge, Mass., 1926).

[30] Rollins gives a few instances (*ibid.*, pp. xxii–xxiii).

[31] There is no modern reprint of *The Forrest of Fancy*, but J. P. Collier argues (*A Bibliographical and Critical Account of the Rarest Books in the English Language* [New York, 1866], II, 32–33) that there were two differing editions in 1579, the only printing date now known.

[32] See Samuel Halkett and John Laing, *A Dictionary of the Anonymous and Pseudonymous Literature of Great Britain* (Edinburgh, 1882), II, 944; also Collier, *Bibliographical and Critical Account*, II, 31.

[33] *Howell's Devises* was not reprinted in the sixteenth century. The modern edition is Walter Raleigh, ed., *Howell's Devises, 1581* (Oxford, 1906).

[34] *A Banquet of Dainty Conceits* has been reprinted only once, in *The Harleian Miscellany*, ed. Thomas Park, IX (London, 1812).

NOTES TO CHAPTER II

The Later Collections

[1] *Brittons Bowre of Delights* was reprinted in 1597. The modern edition, a facsimile of the 1591 edition, has been edited by Hyder E. Rollins (Cambridge, Mass., 1933).

² Quoted by Rollins, ed., *Brittons Bowre,* p. xv. Charles Crawford believed that Breton shunned publicity and fame: because he "had had a tiff with his printer, Richard Jones, he disowned his *Bowre of Delights,* and wished readers to believe that Jones had obtained it in a manner unknown to him, and falsely assigned the work to him, his share in it being but small" (" 'Greenes Funeralls,' 1594, and Nicholas Breton," *SP,* extra ser., I [May 1929], 7).

³ There were no contemporary reprints after 1597. The modern edition of *The Arbor of Amorous Devices* has been edited in facsimile by Hyder E. Rollins (Cambridge, Mass., 1936).

⁴ A full account of this first edition of *Astrophel and Stella,* with identification of the poems, is in William A. Ringler, ed., *The Poems of Sir Philip Sidney* (Oxford, 1962), pp. 542–544.

⁵ The modern edition is Hyder E. Rollins, ed., *The Phoenix Nest* (Cambridge, Mass., 1931). See pp. ix–x for comments on the origin and the implications of the volume's title.

⁶ See *ibid.,* pp. xxi–xxxi, for Rollins's summary of the conjectures about R. S.; Rollins holds (p. xxxi) that in almost every case "where duplicate texts survive those in *The Phoenix Nest* are superior."

⁷ *The Passionate Pilgrim* was probably printed twice in 1599, and was reprinted in 1612. Modern editions are: Sidney Lee, ed., facsimile of the first edition (Oxford, 1905), and Hyder E. Rollins, ed., facsimile of the third edition, 1612 (New York, 1940). For texts, dates, etc., see Hyder E. Rollins, ed., *A New Variorum Edition of Shakespeare: The Poems* (Philadelphia, 1938), pp. 524–538. Background for the name of the collection is suggested by J. P. Collier, *A Bibliographical and Critical Account of the Rarest Books in the English Language* (New York, 1866), III, 98–101, and by Lee, ed., *Passionate Pilgrim,* pp. 19–20.

⁸ Lee, ed., *Passionate Pilgrim,* p. 7n.

⁹ See Rollins, ed., *Passionate Pilgrim,* pp. xxv–xxxiii. Heywood indignantly protested this misrepresentation of his work "under the name of another, which may put the world in opinion I might steale them from him" (*An Apologie for Actors,* 1612).

¹⁰ *England's Helicon* was reprinted in 1614. The modern editor is Hyder E. Rollins (Cambridge, Mass., 1935).

¹¹ See the discussion of Bodenham and Ling in Rollins, ed., *England's Helicon,* I, 41–63. J. William Hebel first urged recognition of Ling as editor in "Nicholas Ling and *England's Helicon," The Library,* 4th ser., V (1924), 153–160. See also Celeste Turner Wright, "Anthony Munday and the Bodenham Miscellanies," *PQ,* XL (1961), 449–461.

¹² The list is preserved in British Museum MS Harleian 280, fols. 99–101. Rollins prints it in his edition of *England's Helicon,* I, 37–40.

¹³ *Belvedere* was reprinted in 1610. The modern edition was printed for the Spenser Society in 1875. William G. Crane (*Wit and Rhetoric in the Renaissance* [New York, 1937], pp. 40–48) discusses the Bodenham collections as related to wit and rhetoric, gives information about their origins, and tells how their sententious material was used in the schools. See also Charles Crawford, *"Belvedere or The Garden of the Muses," Englische Studien,* XLIII (1911), 198–228, and D. T. Starnes, "Some Sources of *Wits Theater of the Little World* (1955) and Bodenham's *Belvedere* (1600)," *PQ,* XXX (1951), 411–418.

¹⁴ The modern edition is Sir Thomas Elyot, *Four Political Treatises,* ed. Lillian Gottesman (Gainesville, Fla., 1967).

¹⁵ The modern edition is William Baldwin, *The Sayings of the Wise or Food for Thought,* ed. Edward Arber (London, 1907).

¹⁶ There were four printings of *England's Parnassus* in 1600. The modern edition

is by Charles Crawford (Oxford, 1913). See also F. B. Williams, "Notes on *England's Parnassus*," *MLN*, LII (1937), 402–405.

[17] Sidney Lee, *"England's Parnassus, 1600": A Note on the Copy Acquired by the Trustees and Guardians of Shakespeare's Birthplace at Stratford-upon-Avon* (July 1915), p. 4.

[18] *Love's Martyr* was reprinted in 1611. The modern edition is by Alexander B. Grosart (London, 1878).

[19] Grosart, ed., *Love's Martyr*, pp. xxi–xxiv. It has been suggested that the poem was an epithalamium for Salisbury and his wife (see Carleton Brown, ed., *Poems by Sir John Salusbury and Robert Chester* [London, 1914]). For other interpretations see Thomas P. Harrison, "*Love's Martyr* by Robert Chester: A New Interpretation," *Studies in English*, XXX (1951), 66–85; and William H. Matchett, *The Phoenix and the Turtle: Shakespeare's Poem and Chester's "Loues Martyr"* (London, 1965). For Shakespeare's poem see Rollins, *Variorum Shakespeare: The Poems*, pp. 559–583.

[20] For full publication history of and notes to *The Garland of Good Will*, see Francis Oscar Mann, ed., *The Works of Thomas Deloney* (Oxford, 1912), pp. 562–585.

[21] For publication history of and notes to *Strange Histories*, see *ibid.*, pp. 585–593.

[22] Quoted in Hyder E. Rollins, ed., *A Poetical Rhapsody* (Cambridge, Mass., 1931), II, 3. An abundance of manuscript poetry, relatively unexplored, still does exist from the period. Searches through this material might disprove the apparent uniqueness of some *Rhapsody* poems. The book was reprinted in 1608, 1611, and 1621. For an account of these and later editions, see *ibid.*, pp. 4–35. See also Hyder E. Rollins, "A. W. and *A Poetical Rapsody*," *SP*, XXIX (1932), 239–251.

NOTES TO CHAPTER III

Tottel's Miscellany: A Source Book for Eloquence

[1] Hyder E. Rollins, ed., *Tottel's Miscellany*, 2d ed., rev. (Cambridge, Mass., 1965), I, 2. All subsequent references are to this edition.

[2] Vere L. Rubel (*Poetic Diction in the English Renaissance from Skelton through Spenser* [New York, 1941], pp. 47–95) allots three short chapters to Tottel poets. See also Rollins, ed., *Tottel's Miscellany*, II, 106.

[3] John Thompson, *The Founding of English Metre* (New York, 1961), pp. 15–36. See also Catherine Ing, *Elizabethan Lyrics: A Study in the Development of English Metres and Their Relation to Poetic Effect* (London, 1951). Edwin Casady (*Henry Howard, Earl of Surrey* [New York, 1938], p. 233) describes the medieval origins of poulter's measure, a native English form first named by Gascoigne in *Certayne Notes of Instruction* (1575).

[4] C. S. Lewis, *English Literature in the Sixteenth Century, Excluding Drama* (Oxford, 1954), p. 237.

[5] H. A. Mason, *Humanism and Poetry in the Early Tudor Period* (London, 1959), pp. 253, 256.

[6] Raymond Southall, *The Courtly Maker: An Essay on the Poetry of Wyatt and His Contemporaries* (New York, 1964), p. 159.

[7] Douglas L. Peterson (*The English Lyric from Wyatt to Donne: A History of the Plain and Eloquent Styles* [Princeton, 1967], pp. 51–86) analyzes poems that deliberately use such precepts and modes.

[8] Quoted in Casady, *Henry Howard*, p. 222.

[9] See Rollins, ed., *Tottel's Miscellany*, II, 107–121, for an account of the Elizabethan influence.

[10] Shakespeare's Master Slender says, "I had rather than forty shillings I had my Book of Songs and Sonnets here" (*Merry Wives of Windsor*, I, i, 205–206), and the gravedigger in Hamlet sings several stanzas of Tottel's no. 212.

[11] See Rollins, ed., *Tottel's Miscellany*, II, 85–93, for a discussion of the identity of the editor. In "The Harington Manuscript at Arundel Castle and Related Documents," *The Library*, 4th ser., XV (1935), 388–444, Ruth Hughey shows that Grimald could not have been the editor. Rollins accepted her evidence in "Marginalia on the Elizabethan Poetical Miscellanies," in *Joseph Quincy Adams Memorial Studies*, ed. J. G. McManaway, G. E. Dawson, and E. E. Willoughby (Washington, 1948), p. 461.

[12] See Rollins, ed., *Tottel's Miscellany*, II, 94–99. Rollins prints the poems in the same order as the first edition, with the added poems together at the end.

[13] *The Poems of Henry Howard, Earl of Surrey*, ed. Frederick Morgan Padelford, 2d ed. (New York, 1967).

[14] *Collected Poems of Sir Thomas Wyatt*, ed. Kenneth Muir and Patricia Thomson (Liverpool, 1969). Wyatt's editors acknowledge that a few of their attributions are doubtful.

[15] For a list of variants introduced into Surrey's poems by Tottel or his editor, see Frederick Morgan Padelford, "The Manuscript Poems of Henry Howard," *Anglia*, XXIX (1906), 273–338. Rollins's collations of the poems, in Volume II of his edition, also give evidence of changes.

[16] For background on this poem and on elegies throughout the miscellanies, see A. L. Bennett, "The Principal Rhetorical Conventions in the Renaissance Personal Elegy," *SP*, LI (1954), 107–126. For the more distant background see O. B. Hardison, Jr., *The Enduring Monument: A Study of the Idea of Praise in Renaissance Literary Theory and Practice* (Chapel Hill, 1962).

[17] The criticism of Wyatt in the past fifty years has been abundant. The major studies are: E. M. W. Tillyard, *The Poetry of Sir Thomas Wyatt: A Selection and a Study* (London, 1929); E. K. Chambers, *Sir Thomas Wyatt and Some Collected Studies* (London, 1933); Sergio Baldi, *La Poesia di Sir Thomas Wyatt* (Firenze, 1953); Kenneth Muir, *Life and Letters of Sir Thomas Wyatt* (Liverpool, 1963); Southall, *The Courtly Maker;* and Patricia Thomson, *Sir Thomas Wyatt and His Background* (Stanford, 1964). An important early article is Hallett Smith, "The Art of Sir Thomas Wyatt," *HLQ*, IX (1945–46), 323–355.
On the early Tudor song lyric and the Italian influence see Winifred Maynard, "The Lyrics of Wyatt: Poems or Songs?" *RES*, n.s., XVI (1963), 1–13, 245–257; D. G. Rees, "Wyatt and Petrarch," *MLR*, LII (1957), 389–391; and Donald L. Guss, "Wyatt's Petrarchism: An Instance of Creative Imitation in the Renaissance," *HLQ*, XXIX (1965), 1–15.

[18] See, for example, Southall, *The Courtly Maker*, pp. 67–77; and Donald M. Friedman, "Wyatt's *Amoris Personae*," *MLQ*, XXVII (1966), 136–146, and "Wyatt and the Ambiguities of Fancy," *JEGP*, LXII (1968), 32–48.

[19] Thompson (*Founding of English Metre*, pp. 18–23) quotes the 43 lines that were changed in the total of 306 in these satires. For a wider background on Wyatt's satires, see Thomson, *Sir Thomas Wyatt*, pp. 238–270.

[20] L. R. Merrill, "Nicholas Grimald, the Judas of the Reformation," *PMLA*, XXXVII (1922), 216–227. This view has not been widely accepted. See also L. R. Merrill, *The Life and Poems of Nicholas Grimald* (New Haven, 1925), the full modern edition of Grimald's work. Critical articles are few; see H. H. Hudson, "Grimald's Translations from Beza," *MLN*, XXXIX (1924), 388–394.

[21] Guss ("Wyatt's Petrarchism," p. 2n) opposes Rollins's statement that Wyatt shows few traces of humanist influence, arguing instead that "imitating Petrarch is a humanistic mode for Wyatt, as for Bembo and the *Pleiade*."

²² For discussion of this question, and notes on the few uncertain authors so far identified, see Rollins, ed., *Tottel's Miscellany*, II, 79–85.

²³ Rollins (in *ibid.*, p. 80) suggests that Chaucer's poem does not seem archaic because it was taken from one of William Thynne's editions of Chaucer (1532, 1542, or 1545). An early annotator, perhaps a contemporary, in a copy of the 1587 edition of *Tottel's Miscellany* recognized the authorship and wrote in Chaucer's name.

²⁴ Rubel, *Poetic Diction*, p. 90. See *ibid.*, pp. 90–95, for an enumeration of several figures or tropes, with examples.

²⁵ For more quotations praising Tottel poets, including several that speak of them as refiners of the language, see Rollins, ed., *Tottel's Miscellany*, II, 120–121.

²⁶ Quoted in Ernest Hatch Wilkins, *A History of Italian Literature* (Cambridge, Mass., 1954), pp. 146–147.

²⁷ See Henri Chamard's modern edition of *La Deffense et Illustration de la langue Francoyse* (Paris, 1948).

NOTES TO CHAPTER IV

The Paradise of Dainty Devices: Poetry and the Proverb Tradition

¹ See the table of variations in content and authorship of the Elizabethan editions in *The Paradise of Dainty Devices*, ed. Hyder E. Rollins (Cambridge, Mass., 1927), following p. xiv. All subsequent references are to this modern edition.

² Rollins argues the phrase is proverbial and is not necessarily linked with Gascoigne (see *ibid.*, pp. lvi–lvii).

³ For notes on the contributors, see *ibid.*, pp. xlii–lxv. Additional comments on contributors and some nineteenth-century judgments may be found in Sir Egerton Brydges, ed., *The Paradise of Dainty Devices, Reprinted from a Transcript of the First Edition, 1576* (London, 1810), pp. v–xiii.

⁴ This statement applies to the poetry of the *Paradise* contributors; Edwards, Hunnis (who succeeded Edwards as master of the children of the Chapel Royal), Heywood, Kinwelmarsh, and Whetstone all wrote other works or translations, now hardly any better known. Modern editions of the poetry include Leicester Bradner, *The Life and Poems of Richard Edwards* (New Haven, 1927), both an edition and a study; Alexander B. Grosart, ed., *Miscellanies of the Fuller Worthies' Library* (London, 1872), vol. 4, no. 2, prints the works of Lord Vaux and the Earl of Oxford. More recent is Larry P. Vonalt, ed., *The Poems of Lord Vaux* (Denver, 1960).

Critical studies include C. C. Stopes, *William Hunnis and the Revels of the Chapel Royal* (London, 1910); E. H. Miller, "George Whetstone—Professional Epitapher," *N&Q*, V (1958), 242–244; Roy B. Clark, "The Earl of Oxford and the Queen's English," *N&Q*, IV (1957), 280–283. Critical assessments may also be found in the introductory material in the editions cited.

⁵ Webbe, *A Discourse of English Poetrie* (1586), and Puttenham, *The Arte of English Poesie* (1589), reprinted respectively in G. Gregory Smith, *Elizabethan Critical Essays* (Oxford, 1904), I, 226–302; II, 1–193. Webbe quotes all of no. 105 (see *ibid.*, I, 277), which combines a couplet read vertically with its extension read horizontally. Both Webbe and Puttenham praise some *Paradise* authors for skill and invention; see quotations in Rollins's edition, pp. lviii–lix.

⁶ Bradner gives a statistical table for meters in *Tottel's Miscellany* and the *Paradise* (*Life and Poems of Edwards*, pp. 84–85).

⁷ C. S. Lewis, *English Literature in the Sixteenth Century, Excluding Drama* (Oxford, 1954), p. 267.

[8] Several settings are given in William Chappell, *Old English Popular Music*, 2 vols. (London, 1893), Vol. I.

[9] Bruce Pattison, *Music and Poetry of the English Renaissance* (London, 1948), p. 164.

[10] In *Romeo and Juliet*, IV, v, 128 ff., Peter catechizes the musicians on this same stanza.

[11] Edwards's poem, which is included in *The Oxford Book of English Verse*, is the only one of his poems for which music survives; the several scores for it show its popularity at the time (see Bradner's appendix on Edwards's music in *Life and Poems of Edwards*, pp. 138–139).

[12] See Rudolph E. Habenicht, ed., *John Heywood's "A Dialogue of Proverbs"* (Berkeley and Los Angeles, 1963), p. 1. Other suggested distinctions and a summary of current usage are found in Richard A. Lanham, *A Handlist of Rhetorical Terms* (Berkeley and Los Angeles, 1968), pp. 83–84.

[13] Habenicht, *Heywood's "Dialogue,"* pp. 1–2, quotes several early Tudor authors to show the unspecific use of the terms in that period.

[14] Chaucer's work, of course, shows that the usage was not new, but renewed, in the sixteenth century. The indispensable reference for proverbs in this period is M. P. Tilley, *A Dictionary of the Proverbs in England in the Sixteenth and Seventeenth Centuries* (Ann Arbor, 1950). See also George W. Smith and Janet Heseltine, *The Oxford Dictionary of English Proverbs*, 2d ed., rev. by Paul Harvey (Oxford, 1948). For a more general background see Archer Taylor, *The Proverb* (Cambridge, Mass., 1931), and "An Introductory Bibliography for the Study of Proverbs," *MP*, XXX (1932), 195–210.

[15] See D. T. Starnes, ed., *Proverbs or Adages of Desiderius Erasmus . . . Englished (1569) by Richard Taverner* (Gainesville, Fla., 1956); Margaret Mann Phillips, *The "Adages" of Erasmus: A Study with Translations* (Cambridge, 1964). Both volumes contain further background in their introductions.

[16] For the text of Heywood's work and an extensive introduction, see Habenicht, ed., *Heywood's "Dialogue."*

[17] For more details on the proverb tradition see *ibid.*, pp. 17–28; William G. Crane, *Wit and Rhetoric in the Renaissance* (New York, 1937), pp. 33–48; and the works on Erasmus cited in n. 15.

[18] H. A. Mason, *Humanism and Poetry in the Early Tudor Period* (London, 1959), pp. 66–67.

[19] Starnes, *Proverbs of Erasmus*, pp. viii–ix.

[20] Thomas Wilson, *Arte of Rhetorique* (1560), ed. G. H. Mair (Oxford, 1909), pp. 116–120.

[21] Henry Peacham, *The Garden of Eloquence* (1593), ed. William G. Crane (Gainesville, Fla., 1954), pp. 29–31, 189–191.

[22] George Puttenham, *The Arte of English Poesie*, ed. Gladys Doidge Willcock and Alice Walker (Cambridge, 1936), pp. 235–236, 186–189.

[23] Rollins's notes in his edition of the *Paradise* occasionally point out classical analogues or sources for frequently used proverbs assimilated into native lore.

[24] See Tilley, *Dictionary of Proverbs*, pp. v–viii, for further examples of these and other proverb types in the period.

[25] G. K. Hunter, *John Lyly: The Humanist as Courtier* (Cambridge, Mass., 1962), p. 265. See also the detailed discussion in *The Complete Works of John Lyly*, ed. R. W. Bond (Oxford, 1902), I, 120–134, and the description in *Euphues: The Anatomy of Wit and Euphues & His England*, ed. Morris William Croll and Harry Clemons (London, 1916), pp. xv–xvi. Jonas Barish reconsiders the accounts of Bond and of Croll and Clemons in "The Prose-Style of John Lyly," *ELH*, XXIII (1956), 14–35. Lyly's use of proverbs in *Euphues* is treated in M. P. Tilley, *Elizabethan Proverb Lore*

in Lyly's "Euphues" and in Pettie's "Petite Pallace" with Parallels from Shakespeare (New York, 1926).

Late in the nineteenth century W. J. Courthope (*A History of English Poetry*, 6 vols. [London, 1897], II, 288–330) discussed the phrase "Poetical Euphuists," construing it quite widely. His concept did not include proverbial content or the parallelisms and rhetorical patterns common in the *Paradise*. Instead he meant a more general notion of artifice, of conscious experiment. He included, for example, the reformers of prosody on classical models, the imitators of Petrarch, and writers using pastoral romance or classical mythology. Accordingly he saw the later miscellanies as exemplifying such "euphuism," while the *Paradise* and the *Gorgeous Gallery* contrasted with them for "purity of idiom."

[26] See Hunter, *John Lyly*, pp. 265–289; Bond, ed., *Works of Lyly*, I, 135–154; William Ringler, "The Immediate Source of Euphuism," *PMLA*, LIII (1938), 678–686.

[27] Douglas L. Peterson believes also that the verse argumentation in the volume "prepared for the mature deliberative lyrics of the late Elizabethan period" (*The English Lyric from Wyatt to Donne: A History of the Plain and Eloquent Styles* [Princeton, 1967], p. 133).

NOTES TO CHAPTER V

The Phoenix Nest: The Miscellany
as Extended Elegy

[1] See Hyder E. Rollins's comments on the identifications in his edition of *The Phoenix Nest* (Cambridge, Mass., 1931), pp. xvii–xx. All subsequent references are to this edition.

[2] For examples of these commendatory verses, see *The Phoenix Nest*, ed. Frederick Etchells and Hugh Macdonald (London, 1926), p. 7. The associations of these poets may be seen more fully in Franklin B. Williams, Jr., *Index of Dedications and Commendatory Verses in English Books before 1641* (London, 1962).

[3] Anonymous review of *The Phoenix Nest*, ed. Etchells and Macdonald, in *TLS*, 20 Jan. 1927, p. 41.

[4] See Rollins's discussion of possibilities in his edition of *The Phoenix Nest*, pp. xxi–xxxi, and Charles Crawford's argument in his edition of *England's Parnassus* (Oxford, 1913), pp. xx–xxi.

[5] Rollins (in his edition of *The Phoenix Nest*, pp. xxxiii–xxxiv) quotes and discredits Edmund Gosse's evidence given in *Seventeenth Century Studies* (London, 1897), pp. 32–33. J. P. Collier had earlier suggested (*A Bibliographical and Critical Account of the Rarest Books in the English Language* [New York, 1866], III, 199–200) that Lodge aided in the publication, since his texts in the volume seem to have been corrected from originals.

[6] Charles Crawford, " 'Greenes Funeralls,' 1594, and Nicholas Breton," *Studies in Philology*, extra ser., I (May, 1929), 1–39. Crawford (*ibid.*, pp. 2–18) also gives Breton credit for compiling *A Poetical Rhapsody, The Passionate Pilgrim, The Garland of Good Will, Belvedere*, and *Wits Common wealth*, and for having had a hand in the compilation of several others.

[7] Rollins, ed., *The Phoenix Nest*, p. xl.

[8] A brief history of the legend and the related symbolism is found in Marion Kaplan, "The Phoenix in Elizabethan Poetry" (Ph.D. dissertation, University of California, Los Angeles, 1964), pp. 4–23. See also, for example, Lactantius, *De Ave Phoenice*, trans. Mary C. Fitzpatrick (Philadelphia, 1933).

⁹ Arthur Golding, trans., *The xv Bookes of P. Ovidius Naso, entytuled Metamorphosis*, ed. W. H. D. Rouse (London, 1961), p. 303, ll. 436–448.

¹⁰ See, for example, Hyder E. Rollins's editions of *Tottel's Miscellany*, 2d ed., rev. (Cambridge, Mass., 1965), I, 203, 250; *The Paradise of Dainty Devices* (Cambridge, Mass., 1927), pp. 81–82; *A Poetical Rhapsody* (Cambridge, Mass., 1931), I, 206.

¹¹ See Kaplan, "The Phoenix in Elizabethan Poetry," pp. 119–147.

¹² Quoted in Rollins, ed., *The Phoenix Nest*, p. x.

¹³ For the titles and a description of these memorial volumes, see Frederick S. Boas, *Sir Philip Sidney: Representative Elizabethan* (London, 1955), pp. 191–192. The *DNB* article on Sidney notes that two hundred poetic memorials were written in his honor.

¹⁴ *A Booke of Epitaphes made upon the death of the Right worshipfull Sir William Buttes Knight* . . . (London, 1583). After 1603, however, a considerable number of tribute volumes are listed, most of them from the universities. See Arthur E. Case, *A Bibliography of English Poetical Miscellanies, 1521–1750* (Oxford, 1935).

¹⁵ Edmund Gosse anticipated part of this view, believing that the phoenix, poetry, was reincarnated after Sidney's death in the lyrics of this book (see quotation in Rollins, ed., *The Phoenix Nest*, p. xxxvii).

¹⁶ See Francis White Weitzmann, "Notes on the Elizabethan *Elegie*," *PMLA*, L (1935), 435–443.

¹⁷ The "places" were birth and infancy (descent), childhood, "the striplyng age," manhood, old age, and time of death. They are taken from Thomas Wilson's *Arte of Rhetorique*, with illustrative quotations, by A. L. Bennett, "The Principal Rhetorical Conventions in the Renaissance Personal Elegy," *SP*, LI (1954), 107–126.

¹⁸ Bennett gives Wilson's list with illustrations ("Principal Rhetorical Conventions," pp. 116–123).

¹⁹ Macdonald suggests also that Leicester's association with the Inner Temple may account for inclusion of the piece, since R. S. belonged to that body and Leicester had been one of its patrons (see *The Phoenix Nest*, ed. Etchells and Macdonald, p. 6).

²⁰ This poem and the two elegies that follow it reappeared in 1595, printed with Spenser's *Colin Clouts Come home againe*. Also included were Spenser's "Astrophel" (his own pastoral elegy for Sidney) and three other memorial poems, perhaps by the Countess of Pembroke and Lodowick Bryskett.

²¹ On internal evidence, Alexander B. Grosart reprinted the poem in his edition of Greville's *Works*, II (1870), 143–147. Sidney Lee assigned it to Greville in his sketch of that poet in the *DNB*. There is no proof, however, that Greville was indeed the author, and the elegy did not reappear among Greville's published poems, an omission that casts reasonable doubt on his authorship.

²² The entertainment was presented at the house of Sir Henry Lee, who had once been advanced by the Earl of Leicester. Hugh Macdonald (*The Phoenix Nest*, ed. Etchells and Macdonald, p. 6) sees the connection with Leicester as a link between the two prose pieces and perhaps as a link with R. S. The entertainment from which the dialogue is taken has been printed, for the first time in its entirety, by E. K. Chambers (*Sir Henry Lee: An Elizabethan Portrait* [Oxford, 1936], pp. 276–297). Chambers calls it "The Ditchley Entertainment." (The only previously printed part was that in *The Phoenix Nest*.) Some manuscript copies ascribe parts of the whole to Richard Edes, royal chaplain to both Elizabeth and James I; Chambers believes Edes probably wrote the entire entertainment.

²³ The modern edition of Breton's work is Alexander B. Grosart, ed., *The Works in Verse and Prose of Nicholas Breton*, 2 vols. (Edinburgh, 1879). Vol. I reprints the poems from *The Phoenix Nest* and *England's Helicon* in a section called "Daffodils and Primroses."

²⁴ In Chaucer's elegy, "The Book of the Duchess," the grieving knight tells of losing

his queen in a chess game with Fortune (ll. 618–669). One of Surrey's poems in *Tottel's Miscellany* (I, 20–21) uses chess terms in vowing to win a disdainful lady: "Although I had a check / To geve the mate is hard." Neither explores implications of the chess metaphor as fully as Breton, or uses it for the world of public affairs.

[25] Charles Crawford, however, believed that Breton wrote this poem (" 'Greene's Funeralls' and Breton," p. 15) and J. P. Collier (*Seven English Poetical Miscellanies* [London, 1867], p. ix) found it unlike Greene's work, though he called it "the finest and most original performance in the volume."

[26] See the notes to Lodge's poems in Rollins, ed., *The Phoenix Nest.* See also Alice Walker, "Italian Sources of Lyrics of Thomas Lodge," *MLR*, XXII (1927), 75–79; L. E. Kastner, "Thomas Lodge as an Imitator of the Italian Poets," *MLR*, II (1906–07), 155–161; and L. E. Kastner, "Thomas Lodge as an Imitator of the French Poets," *The Athenaeum*, 22 Oct. 1904, pp. 552–553, and 29 Oct. 1904, p. 591. The modern edition of Lodge is *The Complete Works of Thomas Lodge,* printed for the Hunterian Club, 4 vols. (1883; repr. New York, 1966).

[27] See "Set me wheras the sunne doth parche the grene" (Rollins, ed., *Tottel's Miscellany,* I, 11). Rollins has not numbered the poems in his edition of *The Phoenix Nest;* in his system a reference, such as 90:6, gives the modern (not the original) pagination, at the bottom of the page, and the line number. Nearly all the poems in the second section of *The Phoenix Nest* are untitled.

[28] For more details and for identifications see Rollins, ed., *The Phoenix Nest*, p. xl, and *passim* throughout his note.

[29] See Rollins, ed., *Tottel's Miscellany,* I, 4, 10.

[30] The ship figure is of course Petrarchan in source. Compare Wyatt's well-known translation of Petrarch in Rollins, ed., *Tottel's Miscellany,* I, 38: "My galley charged with forgetfulnesse."

[31] See Rollins, ed., *The Phoenix Nest,* p. 157.

[32] See *ibid.,* p. 160.

NOTES TO CHAPTER VI

England's Helicon: Music and Poetry
in a Pastoral Anthology

[1] E. K. Chambers, "The English Pastoral," in *Sir Thomas Wyatt and Some Collected Studies* (London, 1933), p. 163. Hallett Smith agrees: "It is the purest of the pastoral forms and the one in which Elizabethan style and manner are most clearly evident" (*Elizabethan Poetry: A Study in Conventions, Meaning, and Expression* [Cambridge, Mass., 1952], p. 31).

[2] Hyder E. Rollins prints the Davison list, with comments, in his edition of *England's Helicon* (Cambridge, Mass., 1935), II, 36–41. All subsequent references are to this edition.

[3] For notes on the authors see *ibid.,* pp. 23–36.

[4] This information is summarized in *ibid.,* pp. 41–63.

[5] E. H. Fellowes has collected the poetic texts of most of the madrigal collections and songbooks printed in England between 1588 and 1632 (*English Madrigal Verse, 1588–1632,* 3d ed., rev. and enl. Frederick W. Sternfeld and David Greer [Oxford, 1967]).

[6] Chambers, "English Pastoral," p. 163. For a history of English pastoral, its origins and main elements, see Walter W. Greg, *Pastoral Poetry and Pastoral Drama* (London, 1906), pp. 78–140, and all of Chambers's essay, pp. 146–180.

[7] Quoted in Rollins, ed., *England's Helicon*, II, 94. See Rollins's notes for other contexts, although he does not give them all.

[8] Greg, *Pastoral Poetry*, p. 67.

[9] Chambers, "English Pastoral," pp. 165–172.

[10] Smith, *Elizabethan Poetry*, pp. 10, 31.

[11] Frank Kermode, ed., *English Pastoral Poetry: From the Beginnings to Marvell* (London, 1952), p. 19.

[12] Edward W. Taylor reviews a variety of attitudes in *Nature and Art in Renaissance Literature* (New York, 1964), pp. 1–37.

[13] Quoted from J. William Hebel, ed., *The Works of Michael Drayton*, 5 vols. (Oxford, 1931–1941), V, 4. See Dorothy Schuchman McCoy, *Tradition and Convention: A Study of Periphrasis in English Pastoral Poetry from 1557–1715* (The Hague, 1965), for an analysis of traditional rhetorical theory somewhat narrowly related to pastoral poetry.

[14] William Empson, *English Pastoral Poetry* (New York, 1938).

[15] Douglas Bush, *Mythology and the Renaissance Tradition in English Poetry* (1932; repr. New York, 1963), p. 225.

[16] For a related, wider discussion of music as image in Renaissance poetry, see John Hollander, *The Untuning of the Sky: Ideas of Music in English Poetry, 1500–1700* (Princeton, 1961), pp. 122–145.

[17] For a discussion of these and other pastoral poems complimenting Elizabeth, see Elkin Calhoun Wilson, "Fayre Elisa, Queene of Shepheardes All," in *England's Eliza* (Cambridge, Mass., 1939), pp. 126–166.

[18] The poem is the introduction to the Astrophel elegy. The elegy itself, omitted here, appeared with this poem in the 1595 printing of Spenser's *Colin Clouts Come home againe.*

[19] See Rollins, ed., *England's Helicon*, II, 180, for comment on this belief.

[20] See E. H. Fellowes, *The English Madrigal* (London, 1925), p. 66, for a partial list of poets whose words were set as madrigals.

[21] For further discussion of form and performance, see Fellowes, *English Madrigal Verse*, pp. vii–xxi. Despite its title, Fellowes's volume prints lyrics from both the madrigal and lute song sets. On the madrigal, see also two works by E. H. Fellowes: *English Madrigal Composers* (Oxford, 1921), and *The English Madrigal*. For the air, see Peter Warlock, *The English Ayre* (London, 1926).

[22] See Fellowes, *English Madrigal Composers*, p. 41, for a chronological list of strictly madrigalian sets, 1588–1627. Each book commonly contained about twenty pieces, infrequently more. See also E. H. Fellowes, *William Byrd* (Oxford, 1936). Fellowes has published the words and music of practically all English madrigals, printed in score, in *The English Madrigal School*, 36 vols. (London, 1913–1914). This series, renamed *The English Madrigalists*, is currently being revised and enlarged by Thurston Dart.

[23] On the composers and their work, see Fellowes, *English Madrigal Composers*, pp. 304–328, and Warlock, *The English Ayre*. Warlock (pp. 137–140) adds a chronological table of literary and musical publications from 1588 to 1626 (the death of Dowland), including the important songbooks of both kinds. Fellowes's series of scores, *English School of Lutenist Song-writers*, 31 vols. (London, 1920–1932), is being revised by Thurston Dart as *The English Lute-Songs*.

[24] See R. W. Ingram, "Words and Music," in *Elizabethan Poetry*, Stratford-upon-Avon Studies, no. 2 (London, 1960), pp. 131–132. See also M. C. Boyd, *Elizabethan Music and Musical Criticism* (Philadelphia, 1940).

[25] Bruce Pattison, *Music and Poetry of the English Renaissance* (London, 1948), pp. 61, 75. See Pattison's entire chapter, "The New Poetry and Music," pp. 61–75.

[26] Ingram, *Elizabethan Poetry*, p. 148.

[27] John Stevens, "The Elizabethan Madrigal," in *Essays and Studies* (London, 1958), pp. 28, 37.

[28] Catherine Ing, *Elizabethan Lyrics: A Study in the Development of English Metres and Their Relation to Poetic Effect* (London, 1951), p. 147. Miss Ing's generalization is more appropriate for the later miscellanies, since the early ones often show little metrical innovation.

[29] Pattison, *Music and Poetry*, p. 76. See also Walter R. Davis, "Melodic and Poetic Structure: The Examples of Campion and Dowland," *Criticism: A Quarterly for Literature and the Arts*, IV (1962), 89–107.

[30] For discussion and wider illustration of these characteristics, see Pattison, *Music and Poetry*, pp. 76–88, and Ing, *Elizabethan Lyrics*, pp. 107–150.

[31] These elements are treated in the passages in Pattison and Ing cited in n. 30, and also in Wilfrid Mellers, "Words and Music in Elizabethan England," in *The Age of Shakespeare*, Pelican Guide to English Literature, ed. Boris Ford, II (London, 1956), 400–401.

[32] Qouted in Mellers, "Words and Music," p. 390.

[33] *A Plain and Easy Introduction to Practical Music*, ed. R. Alex Harman (London, 1952), pp. 290–292. Morley gives extensive technical advice on how to achieve these ends. Harman's edition transcribes all musical examples into modern notation, although he includes some in the original form as well. A facsimile edition of Morley's work, no. 14 of the Shakespeare Association Facsimiles, was published in London in 1937.

[34] John Stevens, for example, maintains ("Elizabethan Madrigal," pp. 24–25) that a composer could and did use any words at all: old poems (antedating the Elizabethan musical renaissance), poems already published as "literature" (Sidney sonnets, stanzas from *The Faerie Queene*), even doggerel, moral reflective verse, argumentative conceits, etc. But these poetic forms had had a prior existence, and their appearance with music does not invalidate the musical influence on the brief, simple lyric.

[35] See Auden's introduction to *An Elizabethan Song Book*, ed. Noah Greenberg, W. H. Auden, and Chester Kallman (Garden City, New York, 1955), pp. ix–x.

[36] See Edward Doughtie, "Words for Music: Simplicity and Complexity in the Elizabethan Air," *Rice University Studies*, LI (1965), 4–5.

NOTES TO CHAPTER VII

The Miscellanies and the Age

[1] Timothe Kendall, *Flowers of Epigrams*, repr. for Spenser Society (London, 1874), p. 9.

[2] See an account of related circumstances in J. W. Saunders, "The Facade of Morality," *ELH*, XIX (1952), 81–114.

[3] In striking contrast are the twenty-one imperial anthologies of Japan, commissioned by the emperors from the eighth century to the mid-fourteenth. These poetic sequences contained a small number of very short forms; with the constancy of these forms they developed two integrating principles more complex and unifying than any Western conventions. The two were progression (e.g., in seasons or in love affairs) and association (usually of imagery, linking a poem with its neighbors). The techniques are analyzed by Konishi Jin'ichi, Robert H. Brower, and Earl Miner, "Association and Progression: Principles of Integration in Anthologies and Sequences of Japanese Court Poetry, A.D. 900–1350," *Harvard Journal of Asiatic Studies*, XXI (1958), 67–127. Brower and Miner (*Japanese Court Poetry* [London, 1962], p. 321) continue

the discussion: "No Western anthology we know of bears the remotest resemblance to this structure. . . . The West has not made the anthology itself a form for esthetic pleasure." In praising the *Shinkokinshu,* compiled ca. 1206, as the best ordered of all, they maintain (*ibid.,* p. 323) that, beside it, such Elizabethan collections as *Tottel's Miscellany* seem "chaotic and almost ill-bred."

INDEX

INDEX